ENDORS

Ray Hughes, my close friend and often co-speaker, called me a while back and shared his experience with harpist Michael-David. Ray has the unique consciousness of true worship and spiritual position for psalmists creating the sounds and music that Yahweh inhabits! I immediately called Michael and encouraged him and his wife, Zsiporah, to meet with me at the home of Johnny Berguson in Pennsylvania, founder and president of Kingdom, Inc. When we met, all that Ray Hughes had said and much more regarding Michael-David's music and ministry was so clearly evident.

I have heard world-class harpists from all across the land and several from around the world. Michael-David's music and spirit are so filled with the authority of God that Becky and I, including our executive staff, Reverend Stan and Nancy Patterson, were deeply moved.

Most of you reading this know who I am and know something about what Ray Hughes and I teach. I endorse the ministry, and the man behind this message totally! This will change your home and your future.

David Van Koevering
Elsewhen Research, Inc.

Michael had done a wonderful job of explaining in each chapter what quantum physics is and how it applies to the life of the Christian who lives by faith in a God that cannot be visibly seen. Understanding the truths which he clearly presents can dramatically alter for better the way you pray, believe, and even speak. You are much closer to the supernatural than you know. The door of quantum physics eventually leads even the most skeptical scientists to a reality that something (or someone) is holding not only the universe together, but also our bodies, cells and individual atoms. Along with his teaching ability, Michael is one of the most gifted harpists I have ever heard. He is a skilled musician who yields to the Holy Spirit's prophetic unction. Beautiful songs that help fix your heart on the Lord flow from his mouth and harp with ease. I believe his captivating new book will teach you how to ascend into the heavenly realms, without needing a doctorate in physics to get there.

PASTOR STEVEN BROOKS
www.stevenbrooks.org

Michael David shows us the two great books that God gives us to understand reality, scripture and the universe. *The Frequency of the Supernatural* unveils the mystery of their interconnectedness. Your journey into discovery will be breathtaking in scope, yet refreshing in simplicity. Experience a profound new understanding of God's incredible power and plan for the universe and how this life-giving plan effects every detail of your life.

JOHNNY and JUANITA BERGUSON
Owners and founders of Kingdom.com.
Executive producers of KingdomLive.TV

Michael-David and his wife, Zsiporah, have visited our congregation for several years now. Their ministry in prophetic harp, song and word has *consistently* released the transforming frequency of heaven's presence. In his new book, Michael-David has harnessed the transcendent fusion of science and spirit. Yet, most importantly, above and beyond, the quantum tangible blessing of the Lord is known and clearly rests upon it. TO READ IT, IS TO BE ALTERED. This book is divinely delicious! Enjoy!

BARRY and TONI FEINMAN
Founders of Jezreel International
The Veteran's Miracle Center, Albany, NY
The Miracle Center congregation
Neshama Designs—Hebraic jewelry, books and gifts
The Miracle Worker radio program

While working closely together in ministry, we grew to appreciate Michael David's sharp, inquiring mind and unique musical talents. His love for God and vision for communicating His Truth continues to propel him forward in new areas of ministry. *The Frequency of the Supernatural* is a fascinating work that's clearly in line with Michael's passion for sharing a deeper understanding of the mysteries of God.

REV. RON and ANN MAINSE
President and Co-Director of
Heart to Heart Marriage & Family Ministries
TV Hosts of *A Better Us*
and former hosts Canada's *100 Huntley Street*

I felt the PRESENCE OF GOD reading this book! *The Frequency Of The Supernatural* is a book that answers the cry from the depths of hearts desiring to know more about the deep things of God. The information in this book will restore a sense of wonder and amazement about who God is and His love for us! Rich substance awaits those who embark on the pages inside this book!

JOEL YOUNT
Co-founder of Spirit Fuel
http://www.spiritfuel.me

Michael-David has dared to reveal a truth that most are yet to grasp. When scripture and science can agree, the light bulb goes on! This book is a MUST read for anyone wanting to truly understand God, the culture of heaven and the world around us.

Michael is a forerunner of what very well could be the restoration of the harp and the Tabernacle of David in our generation.

DEREK SCHNEIDER
President of History Makers Academy
Founder of History Makers Society
www.derekschneider.ca
www.historymakersacademy.com

It's a blessing and a privilege to have read the highly qualified book *The Frequency of the Supernatural* by Michael-David. He is gifted in his ability to explain concepts of physics in a delicious way (as he did in his explanation of "singularity"). His thoughts are illuminated to see things in a vision at a root level. He then transports these ideas to the realm that is beyond matter and then conceives the laws of that superior, higher realm he calls, the supernatural realm. This is a very special thing! He goes deep into well established science and into the most tested and proved book in human history, the Bible, to present his models. These models point to the logical conclusion that comes when we look to the wonders of the universe and its causality—God. His discussion of high level precepts appears to not come from this world, but surely, it's heavenly light was given to his mind to share with us. His vision is poetic, full of grace and is filled with strong encouragement. It is an honor to recommend such an amazing book. Bravo, Michael-David! We see the glory of God in you.

VIVIAN CRISTINA DE ALMEIDA LOPES, M.Sc.,
Astrophysicist by the National Institute for Space Research,
Brazil, specialist in optical extragalactic astrophysics and
image processing. She blogs at diariotorah.blogspot.com.br

THE
FREQUENCY

—— OF THE ——

SUPERNATURAL

REVEALING THE MYSTERIES OF
GOD'S QUANTUM UNIVERSE

MICHAEL-DAVID

DESTINY IMAGE® PUBLISHERS, INC.
P.O. Box 310, Shippensburg, PA 17257-0310
"Promoting Inspired Lives."

This book and all other Destiny Image and Destiny Image Fiction books are available at Christian bookstores and distributors worldwide.

Cover design by Eileen Rockwell
Interior design by Terry Clifton

For more information on foreign distributors, call 717-532-3040.
Reach us on the Internet: www.destinyimage.com.

ISBN 13 TP: 978-0-7684-1927-6
ISBN 13 eBook: 978-0-7684-1928-3
ISBN 13 HC: 978-0-7684-1930-6
ISBN 13 LP: 978-0-7684-1929-0

For Worldwide Distribution, Printed in the U.S.A.
1 2 3 4 5 6 7 8 / 22 21 20 19 18

DEDICATION

On January 30, 2018, my quantumly entangled brother David Van Koevering, passed from this earthly dimension into the eternal realm of the supernatural. He was 77, but had spent the years that he was given by his Creator in a burst of creative energies that ultimately was fully offered up to the Glory of God. His life's work demonstrated his gifts as a visionary, lecturer in quantum physics, and inventor. On a personal level, he mentored and inspired me in the spiritual dynamic of quantum physics and in my own invention. Without him, I would never have experienced the chain of events that have helped to make my dreams a reality.

It is my solemn honor to dedicate this book to a great man of God, David Van Koevering.

ACKNOWLEDGMENTS

When you have the privilege of publishing a book you have the opportunity to honor those you love and who have inspired you in your life's journey. It is these people, who have contributed in a profound and personal way, who make a book possible. So, in the time-honored tradition of authors here are my acknowledgments for *The Frequency of the Supernatural.*

I, first of all, want to acknowledge my mother, who cultivated in me a lifelong love of learning. She fanned the flames of my curiosity and encouraged me in my quest for knowledge despite that fact that my messy room looked more like a laboratory than a bedroom at times. Music lessons were provided, even if the discipline that it instilled in my young heart was not appreciated at the time; yet it has become such a dynamic aspect of my life's calling. In our home library, in an era prior to the Internet, the *World Book Encyclopedia* helped open a world of scientific inquisition. Most of all, she nurtured a family where she did her best to create a loving environment where her children could follow their interests and blossom in their creativity. Thanks, Mom!

Next, I want to express my love and appreciation to my precious wife, who has walked with me through the adventure of my life for over 35 years. I would not be the man I am today without her companionship as together we have matured as individuals and embraced the deeper life. Thank you for your forbearance of a man who has focused his energies a bit like an absent-minded professor while inventing my patented electronic harp, the Harpella, and your understanding and encouragement while writing this book.

I also want to give tribute to the late Reverend David Mainse, who has inspired multiple generations to serve the living God particularly in media. My years at the Crossroads Broadcast Centre allowed me to work with this great man who, like a father, offered words of loving affirmation and recognition of my giftings by giving me opportunities to do some of my best creative work.

Though she will not comprehend this, special thanks to my Yorkie puppy Shekel, who regularly woke me up early in the mornings after I stayed up to complete this manuscript. If it weren't for her persistence this book would likely not have come together in a timely fashion. I will always remember my times before the sun was up, stoking the wood-burning stove and communing with God. This is where my best ideas were conceived, but who would have thought that such a small bundle of fur would have contributed so significantly to this project.

Ultimately, this book is offered up to the King of the universe who created me and gave me life. Apart from the fact that nothing would exist without Him, I am eternally grateful for the sense of awe that He has placed in my heart as "I consider the heavens…the moon and the stars which He has made" (see Ps. 8:3). Lord, thank You for the awesome cosmos that You have made and the opportunity to experience You. Thank You for the revelation that You have given me to share through this book. Help those who are reading it to have the same sense of wonder and acknowledge You for who You are, the Great I AM. Amen.

CHAPTERS

PREFACE

The study of the universe has always fascinated me. As a youth, I studied the starry skies with a good quality telescope and was amazed at its vastness and beauty. A number of very late nights were spent outdoors so I could observe a planet or some exciting event in the heavens. It seemed strange to me that all this was taking place in the sky, and yet it passed quietly with so few people aware of it. This lack of awareness was evident during one of the most dramatic astronomical moments I have experienced in my lifetime.

As an international harp instructor and inventor with a patented new electric harp called the Harpella (see www.harptronics.com), my involvement with music, technology, and ministry has facilitated wonderful opportunities to travel around the globe. In the fall of 2015, I assembled a team of harpists from my previous Schools of the Prophetic Harp (see www.propheticharp.com) and set up a tour to play harp and undertake intercessory prayer in Jerusalem during the last of the four blood moons, the only one of four that was visible from Israel. This "tetrad" of lunar eclipses holds particular prophetic significance in relation to Bible prophecy found in Joel 2, so we felt it was important to be in the Promised Land at this auspicious moment in history. The night of the lunar eclipse, our team was struck with awe and wonder as we watched the moon being swallowed up by the shadow of the earth. The thrill of the event was captured in a music video that was produced and can be viewed at www.propheticharp.com/bloodmoon.

Strangely, despite the fact that this event had caught worldwide attention, during our observation and prayer vigil at the Haas Promenade in the Talpiot neighborhood in Jerusalem, no one else was there! The fully eclipsed moon, with its ominous red coloring and foreboding prophetic significance, set early that morning while still occluded with hardly anyone taking notice.

So it is with the spiritual realm. Sadly, despite the blessings available through ultimate reality found in the Kingdom of God, so few are able to take notice and benefit from understanding the physics of heaven. The intention of this book is to help the reader recapture the awe of the *mysteries of God's quantum universe* and point to the realities of how His Kingdom works, particularly as the understanding of the physics of earth intersects with the spiritual laws of God. In its simplest expression, the discussion in this book will help you to understand the nature of the universe that we live in and how this can make a dramatic impact in your life as you come to understand *The Frequency of the Supernatural.*

The central concept that will help to reveal the *mysteries of God's quantum universe* is the idea that all that is in the universe is defined by the resonance of frequencies that are a part of everything. This reality is explicitly connected to quantum physics. It is amazing to consider how this rapidly expanding field of knowledge confirms many concepts that are presented in the Bible. What is exciting about quantum physics is that it ventures into the strange realms of both natural science and the supernatural. We will examine how the world around us is defined and is affected by both natural laws and spiritual principles as presented to us in both the New and Old Testaments. It is my hope that through an impartation of understanding of these laws you will encounter God and see your life and the lives of others transformed, ultimately *empowering you to experience the miraculous.*

INTRODUCTION

Q*uantum* is a buzzword that is prevalent in our futuristic technological world but is also strangely thrown around in today's society in many marketing campaigns and product promotions. This word is used in association with everything from spiritual philosophy to health food additives or even a brand of underwear. There is a kind of mystique that implies it must have real science behind it. And if that is the case, it must be worth buying into!

As believers and those who are seeking our ultimate reality, it is important that we understand what we are committing our hearts and minds to as truth. So we must examine carefully (and prayerfully) from an intellectual and spiritual perspective what this whole "quantum craze" is all about.

Science has much to offer in the way of explaining the world around us, and the field of quantum physics, which at times seems to intersect with strange and wonderful aspects of spiritual truth, is well worth examining. Even though science may provide the "how" of the universe, the Bible explains the "why." However, there is a prevalent pseudo-science, especially in the context of spirituality, that is disturbingly spurious and full of unsubstantiated claims. As we begin our quest for what is ultimately real in the realm of science and the Scriptures, we will find that science is our ally. According to *Webster's Dictionary*, it is the "study of the natural world based on facts learned through experiments and observation." The Bible says in Romans 1:20:

> *For since the creation of the world His invisible attributes are clearly seen, being understood by the things that are made, even His eternal power and Godhead, so that they are without excuse.*

So we see that all that is in the observable universe points to God's "invisible attributes," which are "clearly seen" and attest to "His eternal power." This is such a convincing argument that God says that we are "without excuse" in realizing that He is real! In this regard, it is a great joy to examine what God has made and offer this powerful testimony of the reality of God. As you read this book, we will discuss not only the topic of God's quantum world but how His laws of physics blend into the spiritual and how understanding these laws will change your life.

CHAPTER ONE

CREATION: THE FINGERPRINTS OF GOD

IN THE BEGINNING

*In the beginning God created the heavens and the earth.
The earth was without form, and void; and darkness was
on the face of the deep. And the Spirit of God was hovering
over the face of the waters. Then God said, "Let there be
light"; and there was light* (Genesis 1:1-3).

There is no better place to start our discussion than in the beginning. Unlike any other explanation given of creation in various
cultures and religions, the Genesis account chronicles with amazing insight the timeline of a singularity that became our universe.
When we speak of a singularity, this refers to a single point in the
universe where all of matter originated and emanated out from.

This terminology also is used to define the instance of a black hole where a star has collapsed upon itself leaving a super-dense mass. However, the event of creation spectacularly goes beyond our scope of comprehension.

This massive, mind-boggling release of energy and ultimately matter that made up the galaxies of the entirety of the cosmos would have warped the very fabric of time and space in such a manner that all estimates of how time functioned would be unknowable. In that highly charged environment, the use of the time frames given in the six days of creation lose their meaning when trying to define time as we comprehend it. Time, as we experience it, is very different from the reality of its true nature, which is affected by factors such as relative position of observation in reference to speed and the proximity to gravitational fields. This aspect of time differentiation was wonderfully portrayed in the science fiction movie *Interstellar*. The topic of the nature of time and space will be handled in a future chapter.

THE HEAVENS DECLARE THE GLORY OF GOD

Astronomers and astrophysicists observe that all matter in the cosmos is currently accelerating away from itself in all directions. Imagine, if you will, dots marked on a balloon that is being inflated. As the balloon enlarges, the dots move away from each other. Similarly, as the fabric of space expands, everything moves further and further away from itself. In fact, it has been calculated that the universe is expanding at the rate of 68 kilometers per second. At this rate, the further away you observe, the more space there is that is expanding. This was first observed by Edwin Hubble, whose name is memorialized on the famous Hubble orbiting telescope. This means that at some point, the accumulative expansion of space is traveling faster than the speed of light itself, to the point that the light will never catch up with what we ever will be able to see. This is called an *event horizon.*

Like watching a movie played backward, if we reversed time and viewed the universe, we would watch everything converge back to this single point in the universe. Scientists have called this the Big Bang, but in essence this is the Genesis account. When God said "Let there be light," from that moment on, that burst of light, representing much more than energy being released in the visual spectrum, exploded in all directions, giving us the physical universe we observe to this day. Everything is expanding from one point, which argues strongly for a *causality*—God.

King David declares in Psalm 19:1-4:

> *The heavens declare the glory of God; and the firmament shows His handiwork. Day unto day utters speech, and night unto night reveals knowledge. There is no speech nor language where their voice is not heard. Their line has gone out through all the earth, and their words to the end of the world.*

We know that the vibration of God's voice during creation was not a literal sound as defined by the audio spectrum that our ears normally can hear. In the beginning, the void of nothing held no medium for sound to travel through. And to this very day, there is no air in space to act as a pressure wave to carry the sound. That's why I always laugh at the space adventure movies that feature jet-like spacecraft that roar through the cosmos with loud sound effects. Regardless, at that moment there was, of course, no human in existence to hear His voice. Interestingly, there were some sentient beings who observed this. In Job 38:7 we are told that when the foundations of the earth were laid the *"morning stars sang together, and all the sons of God shouted for joy,"* referring to the angelic host. What amazing music that must have been to provide a soundtrack for God's creative acts. To more accurately describe this act of creation through the voice of God, it was the unleashing of the resonance of God's will being imposed on the new reality of this dimension. All matter was called into existence and set vibrating with the essence of the energy that God put into the universe by His "voice." This is the very demonstration of omnipotence. Hebrews 11:3 says:

> *By faith we understand that the worlds were framed by the word of God.*

So through the mechanism of creation we see demonstrated these "fingerprints of God" that argue His existence. Just like an artist is able to express their thoughts and feelings through their art, the awesomeness of God is revealed through His creation.

THE GOLDILOCKS EFFECT

From my youth and to this day, I still am in awe of the fact that the cosmos clearly runs like clockwork within an astounding number of extremely tightly balanced tolerances. This phenomena is called the "Goldilocks effect." With my wife's permission, I confess that I've often thought of calling her "Goldie" as she tends to be rather picky about things. Like the universe, there is a very narrow range of tolerance that is acceptable to her for how cold or hot her food and drink should be. The universe is vastly more exacting. According to the Goldilocks effect, if one factor or another is not within a certain narrow range (either too much or too little), the very existence of life and the universe itself cannot exist as we know it without these factors being "just right." As science has advanced, this list of factors has continued to grow, so much so that it would take more "faith" to believe that there was not a Creator than to allow for this list to convince you that there had to be a divine intelligence behind it all.

An example of this is the cosmological constant, which addresses the delicate balance between the amount of matter and energy in the universe. Too much or too little would not allow for the cosmos and life itself, as we know it, to exist. In one case, all that is in the universe would fall back on itself. In the other case, there would not be enough to allow for stars and galaxies to form. In fact, this ratio is so narrow that one is forced to consider that there had to be an intelligence behind it all.

This fact was brought home to me when I attended a creation science seminar and the findings of an atheist cosmologist were presented. In this study, the amount of dark matter in the universe was calculated and consequently a significant conclusion was made. In the summary of this cosmologist's findings, he stated that the measurement that was made was so precisely within an extremely narrow band of tolerance (not too much and not too little) that it indicated that there had to be a divine intelligence influencing this balance. Amazingly, as he could not bring himself to accept this possibility, he publicly stated that his empirical measurements must be wrong because, as an atheist, he was convinced that such a God did not exist!

Paul the apostle states in Romans 1:20:

> *For since the creation of the world His invisible attributes are clearly seen, being understood by the things that are made, even His eternal power and Godhead.*

In my youth, the stars and all of creation spoke to me and I was convinced that there was a Creator. I also deduced that if one could get to know such a God, in His loving care, no matter where I was on the earth, He would watch over me and sustain me. And so I gave my heart to Him and have never since been disappointed throughout a lifetime experiencing the grand adventure of getting to know the King of the universe.

CHAPTER TWO

A Quantum Christmas

With every story, the best place to start is at the beginning. So, when we retell the Christmas story, we find its backstory—the setup for the plot—in the book of Genesis and in the magnificent treatise found in my favorite book in the Bible, John's Gospel.

The book of John happens to be my favorite because of how close John was to Jesus; he refers to himself as the one whom Jesus loved in John 19:26:

> When Jesus therefore saw His mother, and the disciple whom He loved standing by, He said to His mother, "Woman, behold your son!"

I deeply relate to John's heart and aspire to his level of intimacy with the Lord.

John 20:31 tells us the very reason why his book was written, and it could be said that this is the reason the entire Bible was given to us by God. His message is:

> But these things are also written that you may believe that Yeshua is The Messiah, the Son of God, and when you believe, you shall have eternal life in his name (John 20:31 Aramaic Bible in Plain English).

So in the beginning of John's Gospel, he gives us the backstory of the Christmas story, which begins before time began:

> In the beginning was the Word, and the Word was with God, and the Word was God. He was in the beginning with God. All things were made through Him, and without Him nothing was made that was made. In Him was life, and the life was the light of men. And the light shines in the darkness, and the darkness did not comprehend it (John 1:1-5).

We are given an amazing insight into just how the "darkness" did not understand or comprehend the plan of God's salvation in First Corinthians 2:8:

> Which none of the rulers of this age knew; for had they known, they would not have crucified the Lord of glory.

The "rulers of this age" totally missed what was happening, and their darkened comprehension left them blind to the Light who had come and His ultimate purpose.

John continues his magnificent treatise in John 1:6-14:

*There was a man sent from God, whose name was John. This man came for a witness, to bear witness of the Light, that all through him might believe. He was not that Light, but was sent to bear witness of that Light. That was the true Light which gives light to every man coming into the world. He was in the world, and the world was made through Him, and the world did not know Him. He came to His own, and His own did not receive Him. **But as many as received Him, to them He gave the right to become children of God, to those who believe in His name**: who were born, not of blood, nor of the will of the flesh, nor of the will of man, but of God. And the Word became flesh and dwelt among us, and we beheld His glory, the glory as of the only begotten of the Father, full of grace and truth.*

This is the awesome reality of the Christmas story—that the Word became flesh. God became the baby in the manger, and this was His plan from the very beginning—that we would become the children of God.

We note that in both John's account and in Genesis, Jesus is revealed to be the Creator and that one of His awesome creative attributes is light.

Let's consider a word about light. Genesis says:

In the beginning God created the heavens and the earth. The earth was without form, and void; and darkness was on the face of the deep. And the Spirit of God was hovering over the face of the waters. Then God said, "Let there be light"; and there was light (Genesis 1:1-3).

What is light? The concept of light is one of the foundational aspects of reality that defines our universe. Albert Einstein's famous equation $E=mc^2$ tells us that there is a direct relationship between all matter (m), energy (E) and the speed of light (c^2), implying aspects of time and space. In modern science, particularly in quantum mechanics, man has discovered that time does not function in a linear fashion. The reality about time is that it does not function as we experience it. The science fiction movie *Interstellar* uses this reality as an important plot element. In this movie, time is experienced differently based on a person's location and speed, particularly in proximity to a massive gravitational field. Now before I lose you with these scientific details, please let me explain as I tie this in to the Christmas story.

In fact, science begins to substantiate what the Bible teaches us about the cosmos. Time for God is very different from our experience. This aspect of God is revealed in Second Peter 3:8:

> *But, beloved, do not forget this one thing, that with the Lord one day is as a thousand years, and a thousand years as one day.*

Getting back to the concept of light—again, it is John who says in First John 1:5:

> *This is the message which we have heard from Him and declare to you, that God is light and in Him is no darkness at all.*

When light travels, it relates to time very differently from us who are time bound. When it reaches us, a ray of light from the other side of the universe only shows us what an event looked like millions of years ago. In fact, to that ray of light only a moment has passed. So, in essence, all of time may have passed for us, but only a moment has taken place for that beam of light.

Take a moment and contemplate that! Time is not what it seems.

In reality, this is how God see things. He is the Alpha and Omega, the beginning and the end. That is why He is omniscient—every thing that ever will be, for Him, has already come to pass. He knows what we will decide even before we, of our own volition, make the decision. This concept by no means takes away the responsibility we have for our own actions, even though it is clear that not everything that happens on earth is what God desires. Our free will is still intact despite God's foreknowledge. It just happens that God is beyond time and knows the outcome due to His perspective, having created the dimension of time itself. This concept alone explains why God can prophetically speak to us and "tell us of things to come."

That is why John 16:13 confirms this to us:

> *However, when He, the Spirit of truth, has come, He will guide you into all truth; for He will not speak on His own authority, but whatever He hears He will speak; and He will tell you things to come.*

Second Peter 3:8-9 further states:

> *But, beloved, do not forget this one thing, that with the Lord one day is as a thousand years, and a thousand years as one day. The Lord is not slack concerning His promise, as some count slackness, but is longsuffering toward us, not willing that any should perish but that all should come to repentance.*

Which brings us back to the "reason for the season." Paul brings God's perspective on the flow of time and our destiny in Romans 8:29:

> *For whom He foreknew, He also predestined to be conformed to the image of His Son, that He might be the firstborn among many brethren.*

The reason Christ came was so that we could become God's children and be gloriously conformed to His image and become like Him. Children have their parents' DNA and therefore display similar physical qualities. Likewise, because Jesus came in the flesh we have the destiny to become transformed, to become like Him because we are God's children. Revelation 13:8 says:

> *All who dwell on the earth will worship him* [in this context, "him" refers to the beast—the anti-Christ], *whose names have not been written in the Book of Life of the Lamb slain from the foundation of the world.*

Here we see that God's plan of redemption was established before the foundation of the world at a moment when time itself had not become its current reality. It was in the heart of God to redeem us even before we existed, knowing each of us individually in advance!

First Peter 1:18-21 gloriously explains the foreknowledge of God in regard to our redemption:

> *Knowing that you were not redeemed with corruptible things, like silver or gold, from your aimless conduct received by tradition from your fathers, but with the precious blood of Christ, as of a lamb without blemish and*

without spot. He indeed was foreordained before the foundation of the world, but was manifest in these last times for you who through Him believe in God, who raised Him from the dead and gave Him glory, so that your faith and hope are in God.

Our redemption was and is God's plan from the beginning. We are not Plan B. It was His intention before time began to call you to Himself so that you could experience His lavish love. In the beginning we see the promise of Christmas. The Lord condemns satan, the serpent:

And I will put enmity between you and the woman, and between your seed and her Seed [in the Bible, only the seed of man is referred to, not woman—this is a reference to the virgin birth Isaiah prophesies]; *He shall bruise your head* [satan defeated], *and you shall bruise His heel [Christ crucified]* (Genesis 3:15).

Isaiah 7:14 prophesies the virgin birth that is so much a part of the message of Christmas:

Therefore the Lord Himself will give you a sign: Behold, the virgin shall conceive and bear a Son, and shall call His name Immanuel.

Isaiah 9:6-7 contains the Christmas narrative hundreds of years before it came to pass. I can't help but hear the strains of Handel's "Messiah" when I read this scripture:

For unto us a Child is born, unto us a Son is given; and the government will be upon His shoulder. And His name will be called Wonderful, Counselor, Mighty God, Everlasting Father, Prince of Peace. Of the increase of His government and peace there will be no end, upon the throne of David and over His kingdom, to order it and establish it with judgment and justice from that time forward, even forever. The zeal of the Lord of hosts will perform this.

So not only has the Lord planned for redemption for us as individuals, but His plan encompasses the renewal of the whole world. This change in world history is imminent.

But the good news is that this transformation is available for us right now! First John 3:1-3 joyfully informs us:

Behold what manner of love the Father has bestowed on us, that we should be called children of God! Therefore the world does not know us, because it did not know Him. Beloved, now we are children of God; and it has not yet been revealed what we shall be, but we know that when He is revealed, we shall be like Him, for we shall see Him as He is. And everyone who has this hope in Him purifies himself, just as He is pure.

That is why all year round we can sing, "Joy to the world, the Lord has come!"

His love has come to us, and because of this we are transformed. We have the hope of His coming, but we also have unspeakable joy because we are becoming like Him. This was the purpose of His first advent! In His second advent He will bring the resurrection of the dead and the renewal of the whole world!

Second Corinthians 3:17-18 tells us of this great hope:

Now the Lord is the Spirit; and where the Spirit of the Lord is, there is liberty. But we all, with unveiled face, beholding as in a mirror the glory of the Lord, are being transformed into the same image from glory to glory, just as by the Spirit of the Lord.

At the birth of Messiah Jesus, the angels proclaimed in Luke 2:14:

Glory to God in the highest, and on earth peace, goodwill toward men!

Truthfully, we have not yet seen much peace and goodwill here on earth since that day. But from God's perspective, His timeless perspective, the work of salvation that was planned from the foundation of the world was as good as accomplished. Ultimately, in God's dimension the Lamb had already been slain. The work of the Cross, where Jesus declared "It is finished," had already made the way for us to become the children of God. The only thing that remains for us, in this time frame, is to say *yes* to what He has already done for us!

THE CHRISTMAS STAR: A SIGN IN THE HEAVENS

Here is one last parting thought on the Christmas story specifically as it relates to the cosmos. As is retold year after year, at the time of the birth of the Messiah there were wise men identified as the magi who had a keen interest in the movement of the celestial bodies. Some assume them to be astrologers, but they obviously understood that the appearance of an unusual "star" signified the birth of the Messiah, the King of Israel. This presents a supernatural event marked by an astronomical anomaly never previously detailed in history.

We read this account recorded only in Matthew 2:1-12:

> *Now after Jesus was born in Bethlehem of Judea in the days of Herod the king, behold, wise men from the East came to Jerusalem, saying, "Where is He who has been born King of the Jews? For we have seen His star in the East and have come to worship Him."*
>
> *When Herod the king heard this, he was troubled, and all Jerusalem with him. And when he had gathered all the chief priests and scribes of the people together, he inquired of them where the Christ was to be born.*
>
> *So they said to him, "In Bethlehem of Judea, for thus it is written by the prophet:*
>
> *'But you, Bethlehem, in the land of Judah, are not the least among the rulers of Judah; for out of you shall come a Ruler who will shepherd My people Israel.'"*
>
> *Then Herod, when he had secretly called the wise men, determined from them what time the star appeared. And he sent them to Bethlehem and said, "Go and search carefully for the young Child, and when you have found Him, bring back word to me, that I may come and worship Him also."*
>
> *When they heard the king, they departed; and behold, the star which they had seen in the East went before them, till it came and stood over where the young Child was. When they saw the star, they rejoiced with exceedingly great joy. And when they had come into the house, they saw the young Child with Mary His mother, and fell down and*

worshiped Him. And when they had opened their trea-
sures, they presented gifts to Him: gold, frankincense, and
myrrh.

Then, being divinely warned in a dream that they should
not return to Herod, they departed for their own country
another way.

There are a number of things that we can observe about this wondrous astronomical event.

In his documentary *The Star of Bethlehem*, Frederick Larson, an
American lawyer and law professor, notes nine specific qualities of the
Bethlehem star as recorded in this well-known portion of scripture:

1. It signified a birth (Matt. 2:2).

2. It signified kingship (Matt. 2:2).

3. It was related to the Jewish nation (Matt. 2:2).

4. It rose "in the East" (Matt. 2:2).

5. King Herod had not been aware of it (Matt. 2:3-4).

6. It appeared at an exact time (Matt. 2:7).

7. It endured over time (Matt. 2:9).

8. It was in front of the magi when they traveled south
   from Jerusalem to Bethlehem (Matt. 2:9).

9. The star stopped over Bethlehem (Matt. 2:9).

From these observations, we can conclude that this was no ordinary star. I remember in my youth attending a special Christmas
presentation at the local planetarium. The presentation suggested

that perhaps the star of Bethlehem was an alignment of planets that caught the attention of the magi. Frederick Larson used the astronomy computer program Starry Night when researching to verify this alignment. Starry Night is an excellent software that I have used personally, but currently my program of choice is an iPhone app called Star Walk. I was thrilled to have use of this amazing technology, which I shared with the members of my team during my observation of the final blood moon in Jerusalem that I referenced at the start of this book.

Larson was originally inspired to produce his movie when he read an article by astronomer Craig Chester who postulated that the star of Bethlehem was a factual event. Using software, the position of the planets and the stars could be determined, and indeed an unusual alignment took place in 3 to 2 B.C., which Chester concluded fit the evidence found in the Bible. He further suggests a conjunction involving Jupiter and its retrograde motion—at the edge of the orbit of the planet as observed from Earth at that exact moment, the motion of the planet would appear to come to a stop in the sky, explaining the phenomenon described in Matthew 2:9.

I hope this chapter has touched your heart and has challenged you to believe in the veracity of the Scriptures. As God is outside of time and space, He is able to intersect our dimension and enter into it at will and at the exact time of His choosing. He is well able to bring about His wonderful plan for all of the planet and especially for your own individual life.

CHAPTER THREE

QUANTUM PHYSICS FOR BEGINNERS

What is quantum physics and why is it a topic of such great interest at this time in history? Why is this subject relevant to those who are seeking an understanding of our universe both from a scientific and spiritual perspective? In this chapter, I hope to introduce the basics of what this amazing field is all about in a way that is simple enough for most readers to grasp. It would take a lifetime to thoroughly study this subject, and most of us mortals would never fully comprehend it. However, even the most brilliant scientists admit that quantum physics is filled with mysteries that truly go beyond the natural sciences and cross over into the realm of consciousness and the spirit.

Here are a few remarkable quotes from some of the most famous founders of the field of quantum physics. To begin with, Niels Bohr was the Nobel Prize winner for physics in 1922 for defining the atomic and molecular structure and originating the concept of how energy in an atomic system is restricted to specific values. This idea of discrete values of energy, or "quanta" (which is the plural of quantum), is where we get the term *quantum physics*. He reportedly said to Werner Heisenberg, "Anyone who is not shocked by quantum theory has not understood it."

Nobel Prize winner Eugene Wigner (1902-1995) was one of the leading physicists of the twentieth century. He wrote:

> It will remain remarkable, in whatever way our future concepts may develop, that the very study of the external world led to the conclusion that the content of the consciousness is an ultimate reality.[1]

Max Karl Ernst Ludwig Planck was the Nobel Prize winner in physics in 1918 for his work on quantum theory as a theoretical physicist:

> As a man who has devoted his whole life to the most clearheaded science, to the study of matter, I can tell you as a result of my research about the atoms this much: There is no matter as such! All matter originates and exists only by virtue of a force which brings the particles of an atom to vibration and holds this most minute solar system of the atom together.... We must assume behind this force the existence of a *conscious and intelligent Spirit*. This Spirit is the matrix of all matter.[2]

QUANTUM HALL OF FAME

The first Solvay Conference was held in 1911 and was organized by a Belgian businessman named Ernest Solvay. Delegates originated the "old quantum theory," which defined how quantized energy levels of atoms functioned (as mentioned in the text accompanying Niels Bohr's quote above), but by the fifth such conference bearing this name, much fuller insights were established with the "new quantum theory," which set the model for our current understanding. Here is the group shot of the delegates of the fifth Solvay Conference, held in 1927. If there was Facebook at that time I would have tagged the people as shown in the image, but all are worthy of a more in-depth study.

From back to front and from left to right:

Auguste Piccard, Émile Henriot, Paul Ehrenfest, Édouard Herzen, Théophile de Donder, Erwin Schrödinger, Jules-Émile Verschaffelt, Wolfgang Pauli, Werner Heisenberg, Ralph Howard Fowler, Léon Brillouin,

Peter Debye, Martin Knudsen, William Lawrence Bragg, Hendrik Anthony Kramers, Paul Dirac, Arthur Compton, Louis de Broglie, Max Born, Niels Bohr,

Irving Langmuir, Max Planck, Marie Skłodowska Curie, Hendrik Lorentz, Albert Einstein, Paul Langevin, Charles-Eugène Guye, Charles Thomson Rees Wilson, Owen Willans Richardson

Erwin Schrödinger

Max Planck   Marie Curie   Albert Einstein   Niels Bohr

Fifth Solvay Conference 1927

Like many of you who are my age, when I was studying chemistry in elementary and high school, we were taught that all known matter was made from atoms. At one point in my life I was offered a challenge by my science teacher, Mr. Currie, to memorize the entire periodic table of the elements. At that time I would have surely been voted the child most likely to become a scientist as I spent all my after-school time in the lab. He offered to pay me a penny for each correctly answered element, but he would subtract ten cents for each error! Despite the fact that I studied the table carefully, I don't recall actually daring to take the test, but it did give me an appreciation for the amazing sequence in which all the elements could be ordered. Imagine, God created everything in a manner that all matter could be defined so systematically. This has left a lasting impression on me.

I'd like to share an anecdotal incident that has had a life-changing implication for me personally. During this season of my young life when I was allowed to spend countless hours in my elementary school science lab (thanks again, Mr. Currie), I performed an experiment that has become the cornerstone of an invention that I currently hold a patent on. I have no idea where the idea for this experiment came from, nor did I suspect how important it would end up being for me. Here is the gist of the experiment:

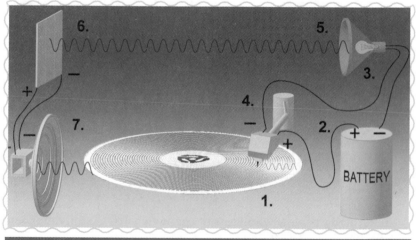

ILLUSTRATION #1

1. A turntable with a record has a vibration sensitive cartridge that a needle is set in.

2. Instead of connecting the cartridge to the amplification circuitry on the record player, one side of the output of the cartridge is first connected to a 1.5 volt battery.

3. The other side of the battery is connected to a terminal on a flashlight bulb set with a reflector to direct the beam.

4. The other side of the terminal on the bulb is connected back to the cartridge.

5. When the record is played, the bulb flickers as the light is modulated to the vibrations from the record.

6. This beam of light is directed to a solar cell (a photoelectric cell) whose output is connected to a speaker.

7. To the amazement of all, the sound of the record is generated in the speaker.

The reason this experiment works is based on Einstein's famous photoelectric effect discoveries. The vibration of the sound of the record is converted into electronic impulses in the cartridge, which modulates the light at the same rate as the original sound. The pulsing light acts like a radio wave invisibly transmitted through the air until it hits the photoelectric cell (thanks, Einstein). The voltage pulse that is created moves the magnetic coils on the speaker converting the electricity into sound waves that are recognizable as the original recording.

This experiment has been modified to form an important part of my invention as follows:

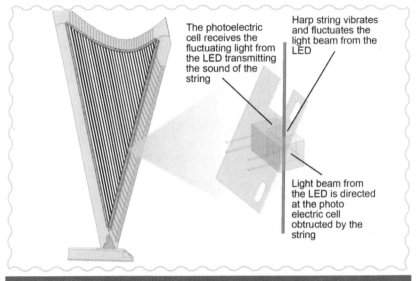

The photoelectric cell receives the fluctuating light from the LED transmitting the sound of the string

Harp string vibrates and fluctuates the light beam from the LED

Light beam from the LED is directed at the photo electric cell obtructed by the string

ILLUSTRATION #2

1. I envisioned an electronic harp that would change the pitch of the individual strings using digital audio technology.

2. I needed a means by which I could capture the vibration of the individual strings that did not have any sound from adjacent strings.

3. I woke up one morning and remembered my experiment with the record player, flashlight bulb, photo cell, and speaker.

4. I said to myself, if I can direct a narrow beam of light toward a string, perhaps the vibrating string will cause the light to waver similar to the bulb in

the experiment and the corresponding fluctuation will be a faithful representation of the sound of the string.

5. When I tested this idea using an LED as the light source and a photoelectric cell as the receiver, it worked perfectly!

The moral of the story is that you never know what seemingly small act can ultimately change your life, and the encouragement of those around you can have a dramatic effect on you. I'm sure that God is fully aware of the circumstances of your life and that He is able to "work all things to the good" on your behalf when you trust Him! As Romans 8:28 says:

> *And we know that all things work together for good to those who love God, to those who are the called according to His purpose.*

In juxtaposition, here is another one of my favorite scriptures:

> *I wisdom dwell with prudence, and find out knowledge of witty inventions* (Proverbs 8:12 KJV).

THE ATOM AND THE PHOTOELECTRIC EFFECT

A quantum leap is a phrase that has found its way into common speech, but it refers back to a basic concept of quantum physics that Niels Bohr discovered. It all started when he defined the atomic and molecular structure. It was around the start of the 1900s that the modern concept of atoms was being developed. As has been taught in schools for decades, atoms are made up from just three basic particles.

(*Atom* means "unable to cut" in Greek, which is a term that turns out to be incorrect.) The electron was discovered in 1897, the proton in 1919, and the neutron in 1932. However, we did not have a more accurate picture until the 1960s, when it was concluded that there are even smaller basic particles that make up the protons and neutrons themselves. These fundamental particles are called quarks. In actuality, it turns out that in all there are 61 known elementary particles that make up what is called the Standard Model. And just when you thought that you'd reached the finish line, they go and move it a little further down the track! The concepts presented in quantum field theory provide the most complete picture of how our universe functions, as now known to mankind. But let's not get ahead of ourselves. We need to first define a few of the basics of quantum physics in a bit more depth.

It just so happens that a good place to start on our "quantum quest" is with Einstein's photoelectric effect as referenced in the description of my invention. In a nutshell, in 1905 Einstein published an article in the prestigious *Annalen der Physik* (*Annals of Physics*) that proposed that light behaved like a particle and not only like a wave. This concept was built on research by Einstein's colleague Max Planck that dealt with the idea that "energy quanta" has a minimal increment of energy now called the Planck Constant. It was in the same issue of *Annalen der Physik* that he released his famous "special theory of relativity" where we get the well-known equation $E=mc^2$. Ultimately, in 1921 Albert Einstein received the Nobel Prize in physics for explaining the photoelectric effect and for his breakthroughs in theoretical physics.

Here is a translation of what Einstein said in his 1905 article:

> In accordance with the assumption to be considered here, the energy of a light ray spreading out from a point

source is not continuously distributed over an increasing space, but consists of a finite number of energy quanta which are localized at points in space, which move without dividing, and which can only be produced and absorbed as complete units.[3]

What this means is that when a light ray shines on, for instance, a metal plate, it gives off energy in chunks.

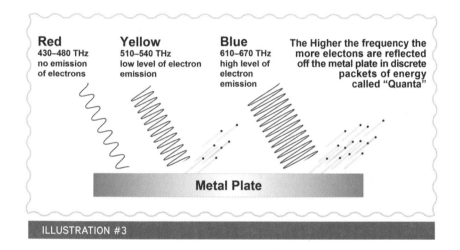

Red
430–480 THz
no emission
of electrons

Yellow
510–540 THz
low level of electron
emission

Blue
610–670 THz
high level of
electron
emission

The Higher the frequency the more electons are reflected off the metal plate in discrete packets of energy called "Quanta"

Metal Plate

ILLUSTRATION #3

You'd think that the more you increased the light, the more energy you would get reflected, but this is not exactly what happens. Think of turning a volume control knob on a stereo. As you turn the knob, it smoothly increases or decreases the volume. However, this is not the case with light/energy. By way of a simplified illustration, if you had a knob that controls brightness, it can only change intensity in steps as if the knob clicks to a predetermined amount of brightness as you turn it.

Not only does the energy in light reflect in steps, called *quanta*, the frequency of the light also determines how much energy is released. For instance, the lower frequencies of light in the visual spectrum (reds and yellow) do not give off much energy, if at all, but the higher frequencies (blues and violet) release significantly more energy. This is also the case with energy that radiates far above the visual spectrum.

The reason light behaves this way is because light consists of particles called *photons*, a word that was coined by G.N. Lewis in 1926. As each photon carries a distinct charge, energy can only be released in distinct packages. Believe it or not, this is at the very core of quantum physics and from this and related concepts we begin to understand how atoms function on a sub-atomic level.

NOTES

1. Eugene Paul Wigner, *Symmetries and Reflections* (Bloomington: Indiana University Press, 1967), 171-184.

2. Max Karl Ernst Ludwig Planck, "Das Wesen der Materie (The Nature of Matter)," Speech, Florence, Italy, 1944.

3. A. Arons and M.B. Peppard, translators, "Einstein's Proposal of the Photon Concept: A Translation of the Annelen der Physik Paper of 1905," American Journal of Physics, vol. 33, no. 5, 1965, 367-374.

CHAPTER FOUR

THE MYSTERIOUS QUANTUM WORLD MEETS THE REALM OF THE SUPERNATURAL

So where does this technical discussion of quantum physics lead us? The Scriptures tell us in First Corinthians 15:46:

> However, the spiritual is not first, but the natural, and afterward the spiritual.

I believe that God is an artist, mathematician, and the ultimate physicist, and as such His very nature and character is reflected in the universe He created. So the natural realm parallels the spirit realm and, in fact, the functions of both dimensions intersect.

But first, the natural.

At this pivotal point in our discussion, let's examine the quintessential experiment popularized in quantum physics known as the delayed-choice quantum eraser. This mysterious experiment illustrates how the quantum world defines the nature of the universe, allowing us to draw a conclusion on how this natural phenomenon overlaps into the supernatural realm.

Before we examine the quantum eraser experiment, we must first consider a simpler version from which it originated. It is called the double-slit experiment.

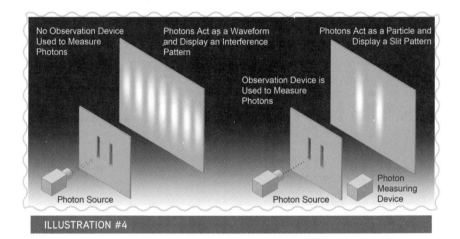

No Observation Device Used to Measure Photons

Photons Act as a Waveform and Display an Interference Pattern

Photons Act as a Particle and Display a Slit Pattern

Observation Device is Used to Measure Photons

Photon Source

Photon Source

Photon Measuring Device

ILLUSTRATION #4

Very basic versions of this experiment were performed as early as 1801 by Thomas Young, but the following set-up was performed by physicist John Wheeler in 1978. Here, a beam of photons is directed at a plate with two parallel slits in it. On the other side of the plate is a screen where a pattern of the light is projected. One would assume the pattern on the screen would simply show an outline of the slits if light acted as particles. Instead, what appears is a series of bars of light forming an interference pattern, because light acts like a wave.

To help you envision what is happening, imagine dropping two stones in a pool. Concentric wave circles form from each stone.

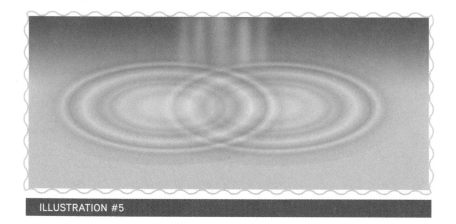

ILLUSTRATION #5

Where the circular ripples of water meet there is a stronger peak in the wave. If a divider were placed in the water in front of the ripples, you would see the peaks of the ripples form at regular intervals on the divider. This, in essence, is what is happening with the light as it forms a pattern of bars on the screen. However, if a detector is placed on the other side of the plate to determine which slit the photon is passing through, the resulting pattern on the screen changes to a pattern that resembles an outline of the slits (see Illustration #4). What has caused the results to change? Only the act of having an observer. Could it be that simply our presence in this universe, acting as observers and participants in the cosmos, can change its reality?

The changing result in this experiment demonstrates the perplexing quantum principle called *wave-particle duality*, where light (and, as it turns out, many other particles including electrons, atoms, and some molecules) can act as both a wave and a particle (if it is observed) but not both at the same time. When a measurement is made in some way, the results change. This act of measuring causes what is called *wave function collapse.*

It is God's intention that our presence here in this universe would make a difference for purposes of great good. In fact, we can infer from the Genesis account that the whole of creation was brought into existence as a dimension where mankind could subdue it, exercising influence in a fruitful and purposeful existence.

> *So God created man in His own image; in the image of God He created him; male and female He created them. Then God blessed them, and God said to them, "Be fruitful and multiply; fill the earth and subdue it; have dominion...." Then God saw everything that He had made, and indeed it was very good* (Genesis 1:27-28,31).

You could say that earth is God's great laboratory and we are His assistants observing the experiment of His love and, in so doing, influencing the actual outcome. Adam and Eve, fresh from the Creator's hand, had the capacity to have dominion; walking and talking with God was very natural for them. You could say (to borrow a phrase from television personality Sid Roth) that it was *naturally supernatural* for them to have clear communication with the living God who originates outside of this dimension. In our further discussions we will see that it is God's "prime directive" to interact with us directly and restore our capacity to influence this world for His wonderful benevolent plans for us corporately and as individuals.

QUANTUM ENTANGLED PARTICLES

As we return our thoughts back to God's mysterious quantum world, one further concept needs to be mentioned before jumping into the quantum eraser experiment and that is the idea of quantum entangled particles. This phenomenon is one of the strangest aspects of quantum physics as it displays the ability of particles that are entangled to communicate with each other instantaneously over unlimited distances. This implies these paired particles are connected regardless of where they are in the universe. In apparent contradiction to Einstein's Theory of Relativity, the particle is somehow sending information about the state of the pair faster than the speed of light. Einstein called this "spooky action at a distance" and was at a loss to explain it.

Physicists are able to pass a laser beam through barium borate crystals and generate entangled photons (and through other means electrons and positrons can achieve the same state). They take on interconnected attributes. All fundamental particles have a property called "spin," which has to do with momentum and orientation in space. The orientation of the spin is determined at the time of the measurement.

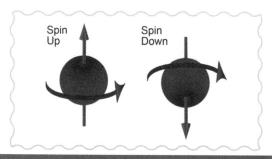

Spin Up

Spin Down

ILLUSTRATION #6

After the measurement, the particle maintains this spin, and the action of measuring the spin actually changes the spin of the paired particles. Rigorous experimentation has proven that when two particles are entangled they always have the opposite spin. We can conclude that when one of the entangled particles is measured we automatically know what the spin orientation of the other particle is going to be—the opposite.

Quantum entanglement is a bit like a pair of socks that I own that have an L and an R marked on them to determine right from left. If I go on a trip and my wife discovers that I left one behind in my sock drawer they still are a matched set but neither of us know which one I have in my suitcase until we check. In quantum physics, this state of not knowing is called *superposition* and incorporates the idea that all possibilities are valid up until the moment of observation.

Therefore, in quantum entanglement, once the particle's spin is measured, like the observation in the delayed choice double slit experiment, the act of measuring causes wave function collapse. The delayed choice quantum eraser shows how the wave function collapses when the measurement is taken after light passes the plate with the slit, and a non-interference pattern is generated on the detector. What is particularly clever about this experiment is that the apparatus is set up in such a way as to see what would happen to the pattern at a detector if the observation is "erased" and the choice of the path of the light beam is set so that you cannot know which slit it came through. The results are nothing less than shocking!

Jesus declared when He triumphantly entered Jerusalem on Palm Sunday:

> *But He answered and said to them, "I tell you that if these should keep silent, the stones would immediately cry out"* (Luke 19:40).

Also Joshua declared as the children of Israel renewed their covenant with the Lord in Shechem in Joshua 24:27:

And Joshua said to all the people, "Behold, this stone shall be a witness to us, for it has heard all the words of the Lord which He spoke to us. It shall therefore be a witness to you, lest you deny your God."

Could it be that in some way, on a quantum level, matter has a lot more to say than we are aware of? In some way, more than in metaphor, do the inanimate mountains sing out in praise to our Creator? (See Psalm 98:8.)

DELAYED CHOICE QUANTUM ERASER

If quantum entanglement isn't weird enough, hold on, things get even stranger as we examine the delayed choice quantum eraser experiment. The objective of this experiment is to prove beyond reasonable doubt that the act of observation is having an influence on the outcome. It shows that consciousness plays a part in collapsing the wave function through an ingenious apparatus first tested in 1999. This setup is significantly more involved than the first double-slit experiment, but even if you don't fully follow the description I will try to make the results relevant to our discussion and bring home its significance as it relates to the supernatural.

Here is a layout of the delayed choice quantum eraser experiment:

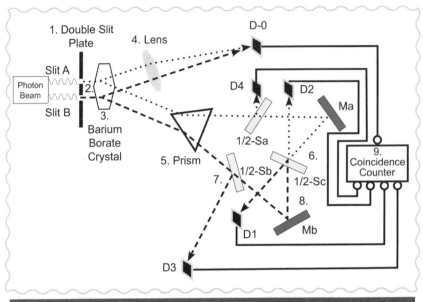

ILLUSTRATION #7

1. A source of photons is beamed into a plate with double slits in the same manner as in the simpler version that is shown in Illustration #4.

2. The line of dots shows the path that the photons can follow when passing through slit A and the line of dashes shows the path that the photons follow when passing through the slit B.

3. In both paths, the photons pass through a barium borate crystal and generate an entangled pair of photons.

4. A lens diverts one of the entangled pairs of photons from each slit to detector D-0 (which is the shortest path for the photons to travel) and a measurement of the photons is recorded in the coincidence counter.

5. The dotted line shows the path of the beam from the top slit passing through a prism directing the beam through a half-silvered mirror ½-Sa, which allows 50 percent of the photons hit detector D4 and the other 50 percent to pass through to a regular mirror Ma.

6. The photon beam then is directed to another half-silvered mirror ½-Sc, which directs 50 percent of the photons to detector D2. and 50 percent of the beam to D1.

The same setup is laid out for the beam emanating through slit B and is repeated as follows:

7. The dashed line shows the path of the beam from the slit B passing through a prism directing the beam through a half-silvered mirror ½-Sb, which allows 50 percent of the photons hit detector D3 and the other 50 percent to pass through to a regular mirror Mb.

8. The photon beam then is directed to another half-silvered mirror ½-Sc, which directs 50 percent of the photons to detector D2, and 50 percent of the beam to D1.

9. All the results of the detectors are recorded at the co-incidence counter.

The results that are tabulated at the coincidence counter indicate the following:

- As the setup for the experiment only allows photons that come from slit B to impact detectors 1, 2, and

3, all photons that hit detector 4 came from slit A; similarly, photons that register at detector 3 traveled through slit B. The coincidence counter is able to calculate the time and distance that the pairs of photons arrive at each detector and their exact corresponding relationship.

- It is not possible to know which slit the photons came from that registered at detectors 1 and 2 as the path, in a sense, has been "erased" as indicated by the name of this experiment. It is at these detectors that an interference pattern is shown as if the photons knew that they were not being measured.

- At detectors 3 and 4 we see the non-interference pattern as if the photons knew that they were being measured.

- What is most mystifying is that the photons act as if they knew in advance which detector they would hit. This is verified as the shortest path forces the first set of entangled photons to register at detector 0 first. How is it that the paired photon knew what would happen in the future? There is no natural explanation for this phenomenon.

There is much debate in the scientific community in regard to the results of this type of experiment and what can be concluded. The evidence points to a universe that seems to respond to our presence in it. It is as if God designed the dimensions to reflect the reality of a supernatural realm where what we see, say, and do has a concrete effect on the very matter that fills time and space. Science is now giving credence to the fact that there is more to this material world than straight-ahead cause and effect. The mystery of God's quantum world challenges us to look more carefully at the nature of the fabric of the cosmos and see that even time itself is not as it seems. Ecclesiastes 3:11 tells us that:

> *He has made everything beautiful in its time. Also He has put eternity in their hearts, except that no one can find out the work that God does from beginning to end.*

It is said that there is a God-shaped hole in our hearts that only He can fill. He has placed a longing in our hearts for the supernatural as this is the natural original state of our souls. This world is indeed God's laboratory—a platform for us to have the opportunity to experience Him. What is significant, however, is in the element of choice that we have the awesome responsibility to exercise for good or ill. It is this ability to choose, a compelling component of quantum physics, that is the greatest gift God has given. It is this innate capacity to have a free will to choose that empowers us so that we can choose to love. For without this capacity to choose we are nothing but robots or animals. Sadly, more often than not mankind chooses poorly and rejects the good God and His higher principles and laws that rule both the physical and spiritual realms. The good news is that we can, from this moment in time, choose God; like the quantum eraser, we can affect the consequences of the bad choices of the past and allow Him to make "everything beautiful in its time." In my opinion, it is for these reasons that people have a fascination for God's mysterious quantum universe.

CHAPTER FIVE

THE INTENTIONALITY OF QUANTUM PRAYER

The quantum reality that our *conscious intention in this dimension affects the material world* is a life-transforming law that intersects both the natural and supernatural realms. This law of intentionality, which is at the core of what I like to call *quantum prayer*, can be simplified in the following four axioms:

1. Faith is the ultimate and highest level of intentionality that is operable in the universe.

2. Prayer is the mechanism through which faith is released.

3. Faith works by love.

4. Acting on the declaration of faith is what gives it the power for the consequent manifestation of faith-filled words to become a reality in this dimension.

We see this fourth axiom clearly in James 2:20-21:

> *But do you want to know, O foolish man, that faith without works is dead? Was not Abraham our father justified by works when he offered Isaac his son on the altar?*

Faith is more than words expressed in prayer or simply a system of belief. Faith finds its expression in actions that reveal your true intentions.

Many forms of prayer exist in a wide range of religions; however, when our intentionality is grounded in the one true living God—the God of Abraham, Isaac, and Jacob—we have the potential to experience something supernatural that is based in reality. The Creator of the universe requires that we worship Him in Spirit and in truth (see John 4:24). If we have an understanding of the true nature of the frequency of the supernatural, then our prayer will be effective and have a dynamic affect. Quantum prayer is therefore not simply some kind of positive confession, but it draws from the understanding of the divine personality who is behind it all. Jesus lays the conditions by which prayer functions with a successful outcome in John 15:7:

> *If you abide in Me, and My words abide in you, you will ask what you desire, and it shall be done for you.*

These conditions are simple:

1. We must abide in Him. This involves an intimate relationship with Him.

2. His words must abide in us. Part of this requires having God's Word as an integral part of our relationship with Him.

3. Then it will be done for us. When we pray, asking what we desire, it will come to pass. Why? Because as His Word becomes a part of our consciousness; then we are on the same frequency as He is. You could call this the frequency of faith. His Word is resonating in our spirit, and the thing that He desires is the thing that we desire (see Ps. 37:4).

Prayer operates on a quantum level when our intentions are founded on a well-developed relationship with the Creator of all matter. Prayer can be ineffective if it falls in the category of "vain repetitions" where the motives of our prayers are out of sync with the faith frequency that God requires us to operate on. Jesus warns us in Matthew 6:7:

> *And when you pray, do not use vain repetitions as the heathen do. For they think that they will be heard for their many words.*

Jesus challenges us that prayer is not chanting some phrase over and over in the hope that we will attain some transcendental state that somehow will persuade God to listen. Similarly, it is not even the long repetition of well-rehearsed prayers written in a book (though a written prayer can be effective if your intention is sincere and based in truth). Quantum prayer is released when we have a conscious, accurate faith that is confidently directed toward God Himself, where there is an assurance that the answer will manifest here in this dimension.

Ultimately, as we mature in our relationship with God, our prayers become more effective. This involves loving the things He loves and also despising the things God hates. That is why the very foundation of the universe is love! First John 4:8 simply states, *"God is love."*

Therefore, it stands to reason that faith works by love, as it is taught in Galatians 5:6. The very essence of God is love, and everything that is in existence is for that very purpose. God desires His highest level of goodness for us, and it is manifest to us in love. That is why when we are immersed in this love the motive for all our prayers is transformed to His frequency. When you are tuned in to the frequency of His love, you have encountered the frequency of the supernatural.

ABRAHAM: AN EXAMPLE OF FAITH AND INTENTIONALITY

James 2:20-21 points us to the life of Abraham as one of the foremost examples of faith and intentionality recorded in the Bible. The event that is cited here, which marks a paradigm shift for the destiny of all mankind, is found in Genesis 22:1-19. Abraham, who is the father of our faith, was told by God to offer up his only son as a sacrifice. What made this act of faith and obedience so poignant was that God had told him that it was *through Isaac* that the promise for Abraham to become "the father of many nations" would come to pass. Notice that God had renamed Abram to Abraham as a prophetic pronouncement of this reality. Remember, when God speaks it has a creative force so strong that when He originally said, "Let there be light," the whole universe came into existence. So it is with every prophetic word that has truly been spoken by the inspiration of the Ruach Ha Kodesh, the Holy Spirit, as it carries the full weight of God's power to transform anyone or any situation.

As the drama played out, Abraham, the boy, and two young men journeyed to Mount Moriah, where Abraham made these amazing pronouncements. Notice first that Abram did not hesitate to perform his task as the scripture says:

> *So Abraham rose early in the morning, saddled his donkey,*
> *and took two of his young men with him, and his son Isaac*
> (Genesis 22:3 ESV).

You can see his intention to follow through with what God has asked of him as he not only rose up early, but also cut the wood with his own hands. Then, in verse 5, he makes an astounding faith-filled deceleration:

> *Then Abraham said to his young men, "Stay here with the*
> *donkey; I and the boy will go over there and worship and*
> *come again to you"* (Genesis 22:5 ESV).

The implications are remarkable. Not only is he expecting to come back again with his son, but Abraham must have believed that God would raise his son from the dead and that God would literally reconstruct his son from the ashes! This supposition is supported in Hebrews 11:17-19:

> *By faith Abraham, when he was tested, offered up Isaac,*
> *and he who had received the promises offered up his only*
> *begotten son, of whom it was said, "In Isaac your seed shall*
> *be called," concluding that God was able to raise him up,*
> *even from the dead, from which he also received him in a*
> *figurative sense.*

Then in verse 6 we read:

And Abraham took the wood of the burnt offering and laid it on Isaac his son. And he took in his hand the fire and the knife. So they went both of them together (Genesis 22:6 ESV).

Here we see the *spiritual entanglement* of this action—the parallel between what Abraham was doing and the spiritual. God reciprocated by entering our earthly dimension and manifesting Himself as the Son, who bears the Cross for our sins. Like Isaac carrying the wood on his back, so our Messiah and Savior literally carries the wood of the Cross on His back.

This is a spiritual principle that also applies to you and me:

For the eyes of the Lord run to and fro throughout the whole earth, to show Himself strong on behalf of those whose heart is loyal to Him (2 Chronicles 16:9).

DANIEL: INTENTIONALLY GETTING INTO AGREEMENT WITH GOD

Let us set aside our discussion of Abraham for a moment and focus on this important principle of spiritual entanglement. I believe that God is looking for people whose intention is to get into agreement with His plans and purposes. It is God's intention that we not only become participants but be the agents by which He exercises His authority in this material realm. It is as if God, in the heavenly dimension, is transmitting the frequency of the intention of His will, but He requires a receiver on this side of heaven to implement it here on earth. He is looking for "those whose heart is loyal to Him," who are on the same wavelength.

A quintessential example of this is when the prophet Daniel began to pray after reading the prophecy in Jeremiah 29:10 predicting that Israel's captivity in Babylon would end after 70 years (see Dan. 9). Even though this time period was over, Daniel could have said, "If God said it would happen, then it will come to pass," and chosen to sit around and wait for it to take place. Instead, Daniel set his face to pray and so became a part of changing the reality of that situation. Not only did Daniel have an angelic visitation, but we see that his prayers were what set the whole shift in the heavenly realm into motion.

The angelic message delivered to Daniel details the spiritual battle behind the release of the captivity of Israel but also, remarkably, is a breakdown of God's prophetic timetable for the end times. This includes the exact time of the appearance of the Messiah and under what circumstances, detailed in Daniel 9:25:

> *Know therefore and understand, that from the going forth of the command to restore and build Jerusalem until Messiah the Prince, there shall be seven weeks and sixty-two weeks; the street shall be built again, and the wall, even in troublesome times.*

It is clear that Messiah would come at a time described as "seven weeks and sixty-two weeks" from the time that the command to rebuild Jerusalem occurs. This topic has been covered in detail in many books and is well worth researching, but it is beyond the scope of our discussion. However, it should be said that in this amazing prophetic utterance we are given the insight as to when and why Messiah would die. Here we read in Daniel 9:26 that Messiah would be cut off sacrificially some time before the destruction of the reconstructed temple.

And after the sixty-two weeks Messiah shall be cut off, but not for Himself; and the people of the prince who is to come shall destroy the city and the sanctuary.

As God is beyond our reference of time, He is able to see past the arrow of time and, hundreds of years before its occurrence, predict the historic moment of the redemption of mankind.

To conclude this digression, I want to exhort you to become so entangled with the heart of God that you take up the challenge and engage in passionate prayer. As you are inspired by the quantum realities in this book that define this plane of existence, the greatest endeavor you can invest in is prayer. It is my hope that you will be encouraged to exercise your faith and see the world around you changed for the Kingdom of God through quantum prayer!

ABRAHAM: TRUE INTENTION REVEALED THROUGH OBEDIENCE

To finalize our discussion of Abraham, we see the progenitor of our faith again making a bold prophetic statement in the face of not knowing how this situation would play out in Genesis 22:7-8:

And Isaac said to his father Abraham, "My father!" And he said, "Here I am, my son." He said, "Behold, the fire and the wood, but where is the lamb for a burnt offering?" Abraham said, "God will provide for himself the lamb for a burnt offering, my son." So they went both of them together (ESV).

Jesus taught us in John 14:15, *"If you love Me, keep My commandments."* For Abraham, laying his only son on the altar was truly the greatest test of his love and trust in God. Perhaps at this moment God is prompting you to lay your "Isaac" on the altar of sacrifice. Too often we hold too tightly to the things of this world, and they become a place of idolatry. Search your heart and discern if it is 100 percent loyal to Him. If there is something that you need to lay down, do it immediately. Do not delay. Be like Abraham and get up early to make it right. When you clear this matter before the Almighty, then He is free to reciprocate your sacrifice and respond in a manner that only an all-knowing sovereign God could devise.

Here is the dramatic conclusion to this historic event in Genesis 22:9-14:

> *Then they came to the place of which God had told him. And Abraham built an altar there and placed the wood in order; and he bound Isaac his son and laid him on the altar, upon the wood. And Abraham stretched out his hand and took the knife to slay his son.*
>
> *But the Angel of the Lord called to him from heaven and said, "Abraham, Abraham!"*
>
> *So he said, "Here I am."*
>
> *And He said, "Do not lay your hand on the lad, or do anything to him; for now I know that you fear God, since you have not withheld your son, your only son, from Me."*
>
> *Then Abraham lifted his eyes and looked, and there behind him was a ram caught in a thicket by its horns. So Abraham went and took the ram, and offered it up for a burnt offering instead of his son. And Abraham called the name of the place, The-Lord-Will-Provide; as it is said to this day, "In the Mount of the Lord it shall be provided."*

So what was the real intention of God behind this strange drama? It was to reveal to us, for all of eternity, the pure intentionality of Abraham who loved God even above his own son. God found someone on this side of heaven who was so filled with the frequency of the supernatural. Thus, He could reciprocate and offer up for all mankind His only Son to die on the altar of sacrifice for the sins of the world. Indeed, God has provided a lamb who was crucified in the very place that Abraham was willing to offer his son.

This example is spiritual entanglement at the highest level. However, we also can choose to align our hearts with the same God of Abraham. It will likely require a sacrifice of our will in a manner that is unique to each one's circumstances, but the outcome for good is beyond anything we could imagine.

CHAPTER SIX

THE FREQUENCY OF
THE SUPERNATURAL

We have established that faith is the release of the intentionality of your belief and through consciousness we are able to interact with the material realm on a quantum level. This is the essence of the concept of the frequency of the supernatural. In the subsequent chapters on quantum field theory and string theory, we will see how actual vibrations in energy fields define how matter behaves in this material dimension. However, the principle of an observer influencing quantum wave function holds true even in these additional theories of quantum physics. It overwhelms our thought processes when we consider the ramifications of this. Our very presence in this universe determines many qualities of how our material world interacts with us. When we observe or measure, this intentionality affects reality. So before we discuss the even stranger world of these advanced theories, let's examine more thoroughly the foundational idea of intentionality. Hebrews 11:1 substantiates this principle:

> *Now faith is the substance of things hoped for, the evidence of things not seen.*

The amazing underlying principles of quantum physics describe a world that is not seen but is very real in terms of our interaction with it on a level of consciousness. These things may seem irrational, but faith functions on principles that, if understood and acted on, intersect our reality and make an impact in this earthly dimension. In simple terms, what we believe in our hearts can change the world around us. However, just because you think something to be true intellectually does not mean that it is real or is a revelation that your soul is fully able to embrace. We will address this in detail in Chapter Seventeen: "Spiritual Cognitive Dissonance."

To influence this plane of reality by our faith, what we believe must be based in a greater reality found in the truth of God's Word. It is also necessary to have an intimate relationship with the God revealed in that Word. We have to realize that what we see with our natural eyes is not that which is ultimately real. We see this clearly in the biblical account of Elijah and his servant surrounded by an army in Second Kings 6:15-17:

> *And when the servant of the man of God arose early and went out, there was an army, surrounding the city with horses and chariots. And his servant said to him, "Alas, my master! What shall we do?" So he answered, "Do not fear, for those who are with us are more than those who are with them." And Elisha prayed, and said, "Lord, I pray, open his eyes that he may see." Then the Lord opened the eyes of*

the young man, and he saw. And behold, the mountain was full of horses and chariots of fire all around Elisha.

Even though their situation looked bleak, Elijah and his servant were surrounded by a heavenly host of angels ready to protect them. It reminds me of the storyline from the science fiction trilogy *The Matrix*. I love the genre of science fiction, as it provides a frame of reference where the big questions of the universe and consciousness can be asked and debated. Along with the moral questions that are often in the plotlines, it is fascinating that what was once scientific speculation ultimately becomes fact. In the case of *The Matrix*, the plot centers around humanity being imprisoned in a computer generated world that is not real. The inhabitants of the Matrix are fooled into thinking that what they see and experience is real. But behind the digital facade, a war is raging and a malevolent advanced computer intelligence is determined to keep mankind enslaved and deceived. The hero, Neo, is a Christ-like character who is "the One" destined to deliver mankind from this evil simulation.

Strangely enough, there are scientists who are serious about the hypothesis that it is possible that our existence is a simulation by some advanced intelligence. An article appeared in *Scientific American* on April 7, 2016 entitled "Are We Living in a Computer Simulation?" In this article, Clara Moskowitz reports that as high-level scientists examine the strange nature of the quantum world they see that there seems to be an unusual design to it. They conclude that there must be a designer behind it all. In *The Matrix*, this evil persona who acts as a designer is called the Architect. May I suggest that there is some truth to what they are postulating?

There is a divine Architect, but His motives are founded in love and His thoughts toward us are for good and not for evil. Jeremiah 29:11 states:

For I know the thoughts that I think toward you, says the
Lord, thoughts of peace and not of evil, to give you a future
and a hope.

Despite our dimension's beauty and very real physicality, there is a dimension beyond our own that is even more real and a Creator who designed it. There is a heavenly dimension that surrounds us and affects matter on a quantum level. There is a malevolent entity (satan and his minions) who is determined to prevent us from coming to understand the true nature of our existence. Jesus came to this world and brought the truth that will set us free (see John 8:32). It is His desire that we learn about the reality and destiny that He designed and that we operate in the frequency of the supernatural.

The process of quantum entanglement involves bringing particles into close proximity so that they take on similar attributes that are perfectly correlated. My mentor, the late David Van Koevering—a pioneer in music technology and the spiritual dynamic of quantum physics—used to say that we were quantumly entangled friends. In his CD series available on the Elijah List website "Quantum Physics, Time, Space, and Matter," he shares an encounter he had while visiting at the home of Kenneth Copeland, a father of the faith movement. Copeland's teaching was foundational in my life, and it became powerfully reinforced in my heart and mind when I realized the connection between my studies in quantum physics and the word of faith stream of revelation. Van Koevering recounts how Copeland had an emotional response as he reflected on David's conversation with him on quantum realities. Brother Kenneth said at that moment that "although he'd taught for years, he now understood why it worked."

For many believers, the concept of prophetic declaration is well understood. In light of what we have discussed about quantum physics, we can conclude that the affect of consciousness on the material world is validated by science as well as the Scriptures. It must be noted that although New Age philosophy has a similar-sounding line of thought, there is a significant difference in the underlying premise. As believers, we are not making declarations about "positive energies" and assuming some kind of universal consciousness. Our premise is our understanding of a divine persona who is specifically identified in Scripture as the great I AM (see Exod. 3:14), the God of Israel, the uncreated One *"who was and is and is to come"* (Rev. 4:8).

Mark 11:23 is a cornerstone verse for the faith movement. Here, Jesus teaches on the connection between speaking to the natural realm and exercising the frequency of the supernatural:

> *For assuredly, I say to you, whoever says to this mountain, "Be removed and be cast into the sea," and does not doubt in his heart, but believes that those things he says will be done, he will have whatever he says.*

We see this theme repeated in similar verses reinforcing this principle:

> *For assuredly, I say to you, if you have faith as a mustard seed, you will say to this mountain, "Move from here to there," and it will move; and nothing will be impossible for you* (Matthew 17:20).

> *So the Lord said, "If you have faith as a mustard seed, you can say to this mulberry tree, 'Be pulled up by the roots and be planted in the sea,' and it would obey you"* (Luke 17:6).

God expects His people to come into a full understanding of the authority He has given us as we learn to resonate with faith at the frequency of the supernatural. Is this too hard to believe? Jesus gives us this challenge in John 14:12:

> *Most assuredly, I say to you, he who believes in Me, the works that I do he will do also; and greater works than these he will do, because I go to My Father.*

Mark 16:15-18 promises for those who *"Go into all the world and preach the gospel"* that the supernatural will follow:

> *And these signs will follow those who believe: In My name they will cast out demons; they will speak with new tongues; they will take up serpents; and if they drink anything deadly, it will by no means hurt them; they will lay hands on the sick, and they will recover.*

At a quantum level, as we direct our intentionality through faith we can aspire to declare a thing and it will come to pass. Job 22:28 declares:

> *You will also declare a thing, and it will be established for you; so light will shine on your ways.*

This material realm will obey our words if we are resonating with the God who created it. After all, all matter was created by God's Word to start with, and God designed this universe to be affected by our words that are based on the resonance of what He has already declared in the Bible. As we allow His Word to affect our consciousness, we become attuned to the frequency of the supernatural and we will begin to experience it for ourselves.

CHAPTER SEVEN

QUANTUM FIELD THEORY: THE GOD PARTICLE

In Chapter Three we touched on the development of the model of the atom that led to the discovery of quarks, which are the smaller elementary particles that made up the atom. As our scientific understanding grew the model that attempted to explain the nature of matter changed to incorporate a more accurate picture. Our discussions on particles that acted like waves led to revelations on how our consciousness interacts with matter. Now, as we begin our look into quantum field theory, it's time to move the finish line again.

Forget about particles or waves. Instead, imagine a quantum field that extends throughout space. For each individual elementary particle that exists, rather than particles of matter, think of unique regions in the field where energy vibrates. Normally, in the vastness of space these fields have close to zero energy, but when energy is introduced, the properties of particles manifest. For each type of field and its corresponding particle there are interactions that take place between the fields that determine the nature of the particles (see Illustration #8). In fact, where these fields intersect, they are the particles! This is the basic idea behind quantum field theory. What is amazing about this concept is that it accurately explains how matter in our universe functions and has been verified over and over again in experiments.

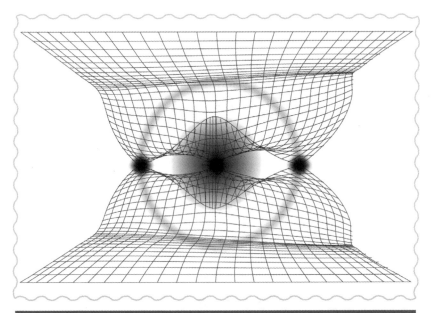

ILLUSTRATION #8

This is an artist's rendition of a water molecule, H_2O. The grid above and below represent the quantum fields, and at the point of intersection of the fields we see the two hydrogen atoms and in the center the oxygen atom.

One aspect of this quantum realty for which scientists have tried to find a practical application is called zero-point energy. Even though at times these quantum fields exhibit little energy, it does not mean there is no energy. Zero-point energy refers to the lowest state in any quantum system. These small levels of energy multiplied over the vastness of space seem to add up to an infinite amount of "free" energy. It has been postulated that this energy could be harnessed to power spacecraft as well as any other device we can imagine. However, on one of my favorite YouTube channels, PBS Space Time, in an episode entitled "Zero-Point Energy Demystified," the problem of harnessing this energy is discussed. Even though this energy is present, no useful energy can be extracted due to the second law of thermodynamics. In other words, you can't get any more energy from a system than you put in. That's why zero-point energy devices won't work despite the numerous hyped-up theories widely found on the Internet. Here, sound science and discernment is called for. (There is more to be said on this topic in Chapter Eighteen: "The Quantum Counterfeit.")

Returning to our discussion of quantum field theory, particles can come into existence at any point in space where energy is present, due to Einstein's equation $E=mc^2$, which defines mass and energy equivalence. Quantum fields can converge and matter can manifest, not from completely *nothing* but converted from energy. However, the equation implies that it would take a huge amount of energy to yield a small amount of mass. This equivalence is evident when an atom bomb or a nuclear reactor, in a fission reaction, releases a huge amount of energy with just a small amount of nuclear material. This is also seen when two elements fuse together in a fusion reaction as seen in stars and our own sun.

When God called all matter into existence, He infused matter with a vast amount of energy. This phenomenon can also be observed when calculating the overall weight of a molecule. If you add the known weight of the protons and neutrons in a molecule, the actual measured weight is usually less than the sum of these parts. The mass that is missing is called the *mass defect* and corresponds to the energy that was released when the nucleus was formed. This property of matter is related to the *nuclear binding energy*—the force that holds everything together.

This brings to mind the scripture that refers to Jesus in Colossians 1:16-17:

> *For by Him all things were created that are in heaven and that are on earth, visible and invisible, whether thrones or dominions or principalities or powers. All things were created through Him and for Him. And He is before all things, and in Him all things consist.*

This is a profound claim that the Scriptures are declaring about the man Jesus. It not only declares His divinity but explains that He is the Maker of all things. In fact, He pre-existed before anything was made. However, this remarkable statement also affirms that "*in Him all things consist.*" You could say that He holds all things together. John 1:3 expands on this thought:

> *All things were made through Him, and without Him nothing was made that was made.*

It is my conviction that it is His Word that holds the universe together and that the vibration of His all-powerful voice is in the form of a kind of high and holy song. One of my harp students who came to my School of the Prophetic Harp (the year that we recorded my 13-disc DVD series for the entire teaching from the school in Israel) is a man of God named Dr. Mike Yeager. He told me that he had had an open vision in which he saw in the heavenly dimension that the Lord was singing a song that was sustaining the very existence of the universe. I concur.

What does all this have to do with quantum physics? For those who have no faith, the discussion quickly ends. However, for those of us who base our belief in the Creator as presented in the Bible, here we see how science seems to describe the very essence of the omnipotence of God. Once again, the lines between the natural realm and the supernatural intersect in a marvelous way.

THE GOD PARTICLE

As the Standard Model of particle physics was developed, all the particles that were theorized to exist were discovered except a final elusive particle that has come to be described as "The God Particle." This particle and its corresponding field allude to the amazing God-like qualities that explain how matter consists. In the 1960s, the physicist Dr. Peter Higgs, who this particle and field is ultimately named after, theorized that such a particle must exist.

One has to smile when scientists are compelled to use words that verge on implications of the divine. It was Nobel laureate Leon Lederman who coined this phrase in his book *The God Particle: If the Universe Is the Answer, What Is the Question?* Lederman's book explains how the Higgs field provides a mechanism for matter to be held together and actually gives matter mass. He describes the Higgs field in terms that are similar to the antiquated pre-1900s theory of an "aether," which attempted to explain the nature of gravity and light.

The Higgs field is strangely reminiscent of God's attribute of being *omnipresent*. We read in the Scriptures:

> *For in him we live, and move, and have our being; as certain also of your own poets have said, For we are also his offspring* (Acts 17:28 KJV).

Here Paul the apostle borrows from the Greek poet Epimenides and from the *Phaenomena* of Aratus in order to persuade the Athenians to turn from idolatry using popular writings from their own culture. The idea of living and moving and having our very being as a result of the power of God is implied. Again, this verse describes the omnipresence of God, who holds not only the universe together but the actual fiber of every one of us. As we further explore quantum field theory and examine the Higgs field, which generates the Higgs boson particle, we will see that it is aptly named "The God Particle."

In order to appreciate the unique role that the Higgs boson particle plays in quantum field theory, we must understand the concept of mass. Mass is the quality all matter has that resists movement. The more mass the matter has, the more energy it takes to move it. This is true of matter on a huge, cosmic scale as well as on the scale of subatomic particles. The Higgs field can be compared to wading chest deep in a pool and attempting to move from one side to the other. The water resists the motion and it requires effort to move through it. Similarly, when a particle moves through and interacts with the Higgs field it slows down figuratively, and that slowing down is the mechanism that gives matter mass. This phenomenon is called the Higgs mechanism.

CERN'S LARGE HADRON COLLIDER

When Peter Higgs and a number of his contemporaries hypothesized that such a field must exist, this set about a quest that required the creation of mankind's most sophisticated machine ever built to verify its existence. This truly awesome device is called the CERN large hadron collider or LHC and is housed in a 27 kilometer long tunnel 100 meters below the surface. CERN is an acronym for the French words for *Conseil Européen pour la Recherche Nucléaire* (European

Council for Nuclear Research), and the facility is located in Geneva straddling both the Swiss and French borders. The LHC is a particle accelerator whose function is to cause particles to collide at such a high state of energy that it mimics the conditions found at the first moments of creation.

By way of illustration, imagine taking two mechanical alarm clocks and causing them to collide with each other while using a high-speed video camera to document the parts that would go flying as a result of the impact. With such a setup you could indeed learn something about the construction of the clock from the images of the exploding parts. This is in essence what is happening at CERN, only at a mind-blowing level of technology where the impact of particles causes a collision that sprays out the very fabric of matter itself. It is through this method that the Higgs boson particle was detected.

In a lecture at the Aspen Ideas Festival in July of 2012, just days before the press release at CERN announcing the verification of the Higgs particle, physicist Brian Greene explained the significance of the Higgs particle as it relates to the creation of the universe. Here is an excerpt from that lecture:

> Because one of the issues in the Big Bang theory of cosmology is that the Big Bang says that way back in the beginning the universe went - underwent this rapid expansion, right? We all have heard about this idea. But the Big Bang mathematics leaves out something pretty important which is the Bang itself. It doesn't tell us what would have driven the outward expansion of space in the first place. Remarkably that kind of object, that kind of Higgs-like object, that kind of spin-less object, if you have enough of it in a little tiny region of space, you can show that it would yield the kind of repulsive

gravitational push that would indeed drive everything apart, would indeed put a bang in the Big Bang.

You can see why the Higgs boson particle is so appropriately named "The God Particle." Not only is it responsible for giving matter the quality of mass, but it also could be the very mechanism God used to expand all the matter He created at the beginning throughout the cosmos.

In the documentary on CERN's LHC called *Particle Fever,* theoretical physicist David Kaplan provides us with this narrative:

> The Higgs is unlike any other particle; it's the lynchpin of the Standard Model. Its theory was written down in the 1960s by Peter Higgs and a number of other theorists. We believe it is the crucial piece responsible for holding matter together. It is connected to a field, which fills all of space and which gives particles like the electron mass and allows them to get caught in atoms. And thus is responsible for the creation of atoms, molecules, planets, and people. Without the Higgs, life as we know it wouldn't exist. But to prove that it's true we have to smash particles together at high enough energy to disturb the field and create a Higgs particle. If the Higgs exists, the LHC is the machine to discover it.

I would like to contend that without *God* and the particles that He created, we would not exist! The vibrations at specific frequencies within quantum fields define everything that is in God's mysterious quantum universe. These interactions in the natural realm parallel the realities found in the realm of the supernatural, which we will elaborate on in the following chapter.

Incidentally, CERN is the place where the World Wide Web was born with the purpose of enabling researchers to share the massive amounts of data that this facility would generate. Activated in 1991, it goes without saying that this computer technology has revolutionized the world, and it was CERN that decreed that it would be free for everyone to use. You can still see the world's first web page at: http://info.cern.ch/hypertext/WWW/TheProject.html.

CHAPTER EIGHT

RESONANT FREQUENCIES

In our discussion of the subject of frequencies, there are many ideas that are scientifically based. There are also many popular concepts that are philosophically and religiously off-base as far as the Christian perspective is concerned. That is why it is important to consider these concepts and sort out what is valid. As we address the physics of resonant frequencies and draw parallels to spiritual realities of the Bible, we can learn to discern and put into practice the frequency of the supernatural that can move mountains and pull down the "walls" that challenge us in our own personal lives.

Every object has a resonant frequency. Every atom on the periodic table of elements has a number assigned to it based on nuclear weight that ultimately determines its frequency. This idea of resonant frequency applies to masses that are both infinitesimal and to massive objects like planets and maybe even the universe.

I previously referenced a friend and mentor of mine, the late David Van Kovering. He was well known for his lecturing on the topic of quantum physics and had mapped the resonant frequencies of the elements on the periodic table. His research touched on the concept of using the resonant frequencies for therapeutic purposes as it relates to the trace elements that are resident in our bodies. His supposition was that using the right combination of frequencies in a given environment would be helpful in bringing healing for specific ailments based on these frequencies being directed at these trace elements.

Audible sound is a mechanism by which resonant frequencies can be experienced. I watched Ray Hughes demonstrate this on stage as he turned up the volume on an acoustic guitar fitted with an audio pick up. As he sang out a note that was the same resonant frequency as the guitar and strings, the guitar began to resonate and the amplified sound rang out with a tone at that frequency.

When you tune a guitar and pluck two strings and compare their pitch, you will hear a beating resonance that is the mathematical difference between the two tones. For instance, the A string is tuned to 110 hertz. If the second string you are comparing it to is slightly lower, say 100 hertz, the difference is 10 hertz and you will hear a beating at 10 times a second. As you turn the tuning peg so that pitch of the string is increasingly closer, the beating pulse begins to slow down until the stings are the same pitch and the beating stops altogether.

A strange example of this took place when my wife and I were doing a recording in the studio. We had recorded the individual tracks in a musical arrangement that included my harp, my wife singing, and a number of other instruments in the background track. When we were mixing the different recorded tracks together, we heard an unusual beating. When we played each track individually, we could not hear the beating. Finally, when we played back the harp and my wife's voice together, we heard the beating. Her voice and the resonance of the body of the harp were almost exactly the same. Interestingly enough, she was the one who originally picked that very harp out for me.

Similarly, when soldiers are marching across a bridge, they are instructed to discontinue their marching in lockstep to avoid setting up a vibration that could destroy the bridge. There is a branch of engineering studying "mechanical resonance" that is dedicated to reducing vibration in structures and machinery.

I believe that these natural phenomena of physics give us a basis for how the realm of the spiritual operates. Where resonant frequencies are a powerful example of physical laws, there is an even more powerful set of principles that operate in the dimension of the Spirit. This brings to mind a familiar story in the Bible found in Joshua 6. Here, we find the narrative about the city of Jericho encircled by the armies of Israel with a specific and unusual battle strategy. In obedience to God's command, they were to march around the walls once a day blowing the shofars (rams' horns) and carrying the Ark of the Covenant. They were also to refrain from speaking during this whole time until the shout went up on the seventh day. However, on the seventh day they were to circle the city seven times and give a great shout and a long blast of the horns and the walls would fall down flat. When they were obedient, the walls crumbled and they ran up to take the city.

Was this exercise strictly an ancient example of resonant frequencies pulling down a wall, or was there something else at work? I believe there certainly was a frequency that was released that day, but it was the frequency of the supernatural. Whenever we get into agreement with God's instructions, we will see amazing results. Notice they were instructed to not speak at all during this campaign. Not a word of doubt was permitted. At the final shout of victory, the walls came down.

If we learn to listen for God's still small voice, we can tune in to that frequency and get into agreement with God's plans and purposes. Jesus lived a life of prayer that gave us an example to follow. He gave us the secret to success in our prayer life when He said:

> Then Jesus answered and said to them, "Most assuredly, I say to you, the Son can do nothing of Himself, but what He sees the Father do; for whatever He does, the Son also does in like manner" (John 5:19).

Prayer, in essence, is simply praying what God is already doing. God is looking for those who are praying in this manner and whose hearts are on the same wavelength. This synchronicity in prayer is called quantum prayer.

We read another story in Second Chronicles 20:20-22 that reaffirms the concept of God's people tuning into the prophetic voice of God, acting in obedience and with the release of a sound that was on the "Frequency of the Supernatural" the battle was won!

> Jehoshaphat stood and said, "Hear me, O Judah and you inhabitants of Jerusalem: Believe in the Lord your God, and you shall be established; believe His prophets, and you shall prosper." And when he had consulted with the people, he appointed those who should sing to the Lord, and who should praise the beauty of holiness, as they went out before the army and were saying: "Praise the Lord, for His mercy endures forever." Now when they began to sing and to praise, the Lord set ambushes against the people of

Ammon, Moab, and Mount Seir, who had come against
Judah; and they were defeated.

The act of worship sets up a resonance with God that can move mountains. Whatever the obstacle, when we speak in faith the walls come tumbling down. Jesus declares to us in Matthew 21:21:

> *So Jesus answered and said to them, "Assuredly, I say to*
> *you, if you have faith and do not doubt, you will not only*
> *do what was done to the fig tree, but also if you say to this*
> *mountain, 'Be removed and be cast into the sea,' it will be*
> *done."*

Notice that a critical component to this formula is what we say! What we say not only produces a sound that is heard in the natural realm, it sets off a "vibration" that is spiritual and ultimately results in us receiving what we are saying. This is a truly astounding promise.

How do we acquire the ability to speak such powerful words that have the resonance to change the material world in a miraculous way? When you get on the same frequency as God by saturating yourself with His Word something amazing happens. You get on the frequency of the supernatural. Romans 10:17 tells us, "*So then faith comes by hearing, and hearing by the word of God.*"

Faith literally is created in your heart when you are exposed to God's Word. And when we are exposed to God's Word it transforms us. Psalm 37:4 says:

> *Delight yourself also in the Lord, and He shall give you the*
> *desires of your heart.*

I look at this verse from two perspectives. On one hand, when we delight ourselves in the Lord, He gives us the things we desire. But more importantly, as we are in His Word and discover the things that God delights in, He imparts the actual desire for those things He wants us to have. It's a win-win situation.

But what causes us to at times not receive the things that we are hoping for? When we are not on the same frequency as God, we can't pick up His signal and we can't hear Him. Our desires are not necessarily His desires, and all we end up with is frustration and disappointment in our lives. Sometimes we even blame God for our troubles. Personally, I know myself well enough that I don't need to blame God for the trouble I get myself into.

This disconnect with God ultimately was caused when Adam and Eve sinned in the Garden of Eden. To give a more technologically updated illustration, David Van Koevering (who now has his full bandwidth restored in heaven) liked to say that they lost their bandwidth (in reference to the speed at which data can be transmitted over the Internet). Prior to the Fall, they were perfectly connected to God with unlimited bandwidth to receive God's love and provision. When they sinned (as we all do) not only was their bandwidth to God limited, it was disconnected altogether.

Isn't it frustrating when our Internet connection goes down? However, one can't even realistically compare this with how great a disaster for mankind it was, and is, for us to lose our connection with our Creator. They were no longer reverberating with God. They were no long functioning on the frequency of the supernatural. Still, to this very day He calls out to us, as He called out to Adam, "Where are you?"

Fortunately, this was not the end of the story. In fact, even before the story began, before time even started, God anticipated this moment. As it was first stated in Chapter One, God's act of redemption "before the foundations of the world" had already taken place in the annals of time.

So where does this leave us? We have the opportunity to allow God to be the divine administrator of the gateway to our souls. Please allow me to make a parallel parable between our souls and a computer system. Sin is the virus that has disabled our soul's operating system. It was placed there by a malevolent hacker named satan. It is his sole function to mess up your life (and especially your afterlife) as much as possible. Fortunately, the divine programmer who made everything does not want to you to be locked out. He already has an antivirus software that He wants to run in your soul. The software is His plan of salvation that can clean the hard drive of your heart and restore your system and give you access to the bandwidth of heaven as He had planned from the beginning. All we have to do is allow Him access to our system. If you haven't already done this, just click OK (figuratively) and pray a simple prayer, something like this:

> *Creator, my life has been messed up by allowing the virus of sin in my life. Please apply Your fix to my soul. I accept Your "antivirus" solution that You designed when Jesus died for my sins and rose from the dead to give me life. I give You complete access to my heart. Amen.*

> *For I delivered to you first of all that which I also received: that Christ died for our sins according to the Scriptures, and that He was buried, and that He rose again the third day according to the Scriptures* (1 Corinthians 15:3-4).

CHAPTER NINE

GRAVITATIONAL WAVES: A NEW ERA OF ASTRONOMY BEGINS

The main theme in our discussion of quantum physics has been how everything in the universe can be defined in terms of frequency and energy. Whether we have been referring to particles and waves or energy interacting with fields creating particles, it all relates to vibrations at a specific frequency. The faster the oscillation, the more energy the system has. We have also been exploring the supernatural connections to the physical universe and seeing what Holy Scripture has to say about the nature of God and His creation and how we interact with it. Now we will delve into the latest scientific breakthrough in astronomical technology and see how even the very fabric of space and time vibrates with waves—gravitational waves.

Gravity. It's a very heavy scientific topic (pun intended). But what is it? Frankly, we don't know. We know what gravity does and we find out every time we drop something—or something drops on us! Just ask Sir Isaac Newton, who in 1666 had an epiphany when supposedly an apple fell on his head. Whether it actually fell on his head or not, at least Newton confirms the association with the falling apple and his musings on the force of gravity in his biography. From his writings it is clear Newton had a strong belief in God. Here is an excerpt from his treatise *Principia* confirming this:

> This most beautiful system of the sun, planets, and comets, could only proceed from the counsel and dominion of an intelligent Being. ...This Being governs all things, not as the soul of the world, but as Lord over all; and on account of his dominion he is wont to be called "Lord God" παντοκρατωρ [pantokratōr], or "Universal Ruler". ...The Supreme God is a Being eternal, infinite, [and] absolutely perfect.[1]

Sir Isaac Newton was clearly one of the most influential scientists of all time. His mathematical formulas, whose methodology was often invented by Newton himself, have stood the test of time and are still relevant to this day. In particular, Newton's equations defining the movement of the stars and the planets were used to send man to the moon.

Even though Isaac Newton defined mathematically the way masses behaved in relation to gravitational forces, he understood little of the actual mechanism that caused it. It was through Einstein's concept of time and space that we were brought to a whole new paradigm. What Einstein conceptualized about gravity has been verified experimentally even as recently as September 14, 2015. I'm referring to a brand-new branch of astronomy that looks at the universe in a manner that previously did not exist, utilizing what is called a *laser interferometer gravitational-wave observatory*, or LIGO for short.

A century ago, Einstein theorized that events in the cosmos that involved unimaginably large masses and energies would generate gravitational waves in the very fabric of space-time. By way of illustration, imagine a trampoline with a bowling ball resting on the elastic surface. The weight of the ball would cause the fabric to form an indentation around the ball. Now roll a marble just past the bowling ball so that it dipped into the indentation. The path of the marble would curve around the bowling ball, just as the moon orbits around the earth or the planets around the sun. This is a fair explanation of how gravity works. Now imagine rolling two bowling balls toward each so that they just pass each other. If you time it just right, the two balls would form an indentation that would trap the balls and eventually cause them to collide. When this happened, there would be a ripple on the surface of the trampoline. If recorded with a vibration sensor, you could document the waveform that was detected at the time of the collision.

Here's how the LIGO works.

A laser beam is directed to a device that splits it into two paths with each of the two beams being shot at mirrors at the end of two four-kilometer long paths (see Illustration #9). The mirrors then reflect the beams back to the splitting device in such a way as to match up the light waveforms at a detector. When these waveforms are in sync with each other, they register one with another indicating that no gravitational wave is present. However, as Einstein predicted, when a massive gravitational event takes place, time-space contracts and expands so that the distance between the mirrors and beam detectors actually changes on a miniscule scale smaller than one ten-thousandth the diameter of a proton. This change is enough for the light waves from the laser to get out of sync, generating an oscillation pattern representing the frequency of the gravitational wave.

On September 14, 2015, for the first time in the history of mankind, such an event was detected, ushering in a new era in astronomy. The detection was registered by two twin LIGO facilities—located in Livingston, Louisiana and Hanford, Washington—both built and operated by Caltec and MIT. As the identical gravitational wave pattern arrived in Livingston seven milliseconds before Hanford it was concluded that the source of the wave originated in the Southern Hemisphere.

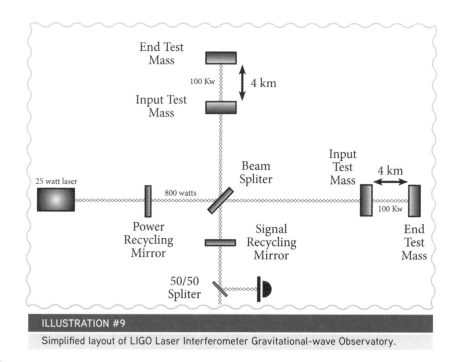

ILLUSTRATION #9

Simplified layout of LIGO Laser Interferometer Gravitational-wave Observatory.

The World Science Festival held a fascinating event that caught a sense of the human drama that took place when the first detection of a gravitational wave occurred. Brian Green interviewed some of the scientists who were responsible for this breakthrough in astrophysics. During the interview of this distinguished panel, they remarked on how the circumstances of this first detection were remarkable. The gravitational wave, lasting only a brief moment, had been traveling through space-time for 1.3 billion years, and the recording of that exact moment was captured only two days after the LIGO was put online. In fact, they almost missed detecting the wave. A technician needed to do a fix that would have shut down the LIGO, but he was denied, and by chance the system was left on. At first, the scientists could hardly believe the results that they were seeing. The pattern of the actual gravitational wave was exactly as they had predicted in their waveform modeling when compared side by side. They declared, "You can actually see the waveform directly in the data. Nature has given us a gift…we didn't even expect something as good as this."[2]

Gravitational wave astronomy has given scientists a new way to observe the universe, and, at the time of the writing of this book, a number of additional occurrences have taken place. One also registered in the visual light spectrum on August 17, 2017—two neutron stars that rapidly circled each other until they collided, approximately 130 million years ago. Not only was the gravitational wave detected in the twin LIGO observatories in North America, it was also picked up at the Virgo detector near Pisa, Italy. Having these three facilities detect the wave helped astronomers triangulate the direction of the wave. In turn, this enabled scientists around the globe to locate the position in the sky to direct 70 separate telescopes to see this event. One of the technicians who was involved in this detection was astonished at how "luck" was a remarkable part of the circumstances. Like the first observation at LIGO, the results were described as "a gift"—the wave fell exactly into the design parameters and each facility was turned on at just the right time.[3]

As scientists celebrate this amazing achievement, one could ponder what this all means, particularly from God's perspective. Is there a message of some kind behind such a momentous intersection of timing and new technology? The scope of the release of energy on such a mind-boggling scale leaves us with a sense of awe and wonder. I believe at this time in history and the advancement of mankind's understanding of the universe, God is revealing to the human race just how awesome He is. As the body of work an artist creates in their lifetime reveals something of who they are as a person, so God, the great Master Artist, is giving us a glimpse into what He is like. The universe is His canvas, quantum physics is his palette, and all matter that makes up the stars and the planets (and even our body and soul) is the pigment He uses to paint a picture of His greatness! Genesis 1:14 says:

> And God said, "Let there be lights in the expanse of the heavens to separate the day from the night. And let them be for signs and for seasons, and for days" (ESV).

A sign is posted to alert us to something important that we need to take notice of. In some cases, not heeding it can have dire consequences. As the heavens declare God's handiwork, the message of the sign is clear. There is an all-powerful God who created the universe, and He knows you and wants you to know Him. The message of the vastness of space surrounding this tiny blue dot we call home is God saying that He knows not only every star by name (see Ps. 147:4), but He also counts every hair on our heads (see Luke 12:7). He knows us completely. His thoughts for us are as numerous as the sands on the seashore (see Ps. 139:18), and He loves us!

In these end times, technology has given us a greater ability to observe God's vast universe in ways never before possible. The timing of the observation of specific incredible astronomical events is indeed uncanny. As we close this chapter, I'd like to mention an astronomical event that took place when comet Shoemaker/Levy collided with

Jupiter. Like so many factors that make life on Earth possible, in classic "Goldilocks effect," the planet Jupiter acts like a "cosmic vacuum cleaner" that sucks potentially lethal asteroids and comets away from Earth. Without the presence of Jupiter's strong gravitational influence in our solar system, no doubt life would have been destroyed here on our planet from a catastrophic collision. Statistically speaking, Jupiter has an impact rate of 2,000 to 8,000 times higher than our home planet.

In the case of comet Shoemaker/Levy, the astronomers the comet is named for detected its collision course trajectory in advance of the impact. This allowed every available observation device to be trained on the planet for one of the most spectacular fireworks shows of all time. In apocalyptic fashion, the comet broke into 21 pieces as it entered into Jupiter's atmosphere, bursting into explosions that released more energy than our largest nuclear weapons. This awe-inspiring cosmic 21-gun salute pays tribute to the Creator of the universe and hints at the kind of events poured out in the Book of Revelation. Perhaps this is just the "pre-game show"—the fight before the main event. One must ask—what are the chances of us encountering such cosmic events at just the right time to be observing them? I believe these cosmic events—such as the detection of massive gravitational waves and events such as comet Shoemaker/Levy—are signs that alert us to the season that we are in, in these end of days. What is the message? Watch, be ready, and pray that we will not miss our day of visitation of the plans of God in these end times.

NOTES

1. Isaac Newton, Principia Book III, qtd. in H.S. Thayer, *Newton's Philosophy of Nature: Selections from His Writings* (New York, NY: Hafner Library of Classics, 1953), 42.

2. World Science Festival, "Gravitational Waves: A New Era of Astronomy Begins," YouTube, June 22, 2016, 44:25, https://www.youtube.com/watch?v=xj6vV3T4ok8&feature=youtu.be.

3. Robert Naeye, "LIGO Detects a Neutron Star Merger," Astronomy.com, October 16, 2017, http://www.astronomy.com/news/2017/10/ligo-detects-a-neutron-star-merger.

CHAPTER TEN

TIME AND SPACE AND THE NATURE OF GOD

As we turn to the physics of time and space, science verifies how time is affected by factors such as speed relative to other objects as well as proximity to gravitational fields. We previously referenced the movie *Interstellar,* in which a spacecraft is being sent to a distant solar system in hopes of finding a new home for mankind. In the movie, time is running out for planet Earth as its ecosystem is failing. A new world is being considered for colonization, but it is situated close to the strong gravitational field of a nearby black hole. Their time for exploration is limited and further exacerbated by the fact that time slows down for the astronauts as they near the planet. Ultimately, the protagonist returns to find that his daughter has aged far past him. Although this is science fiction, if space travel of this nature were possible, these time factors would be a reality.

Strangely enough, *time dilation*, as this phenomenon is called, is something that plays an important role in our everyday lives, especially if you use a GPS. This concept states that the closer you are to a strong gravitational field the more time slows down for you, while something further away is less influenced by that gravitational field. GPS technologies need to make time dilation adjustments in the math when calculating our location because they rely on satellites that are high above the earth. If time dilation is not taken into consideration, your GPS would calculate your position incorrectly!

All mass has gravity; and gravity, by nature, warps space-time. Not only is time affected by gravity, but light actually bends around matter. Remember our bowling ball on a trampoline illustration. Even though photons (light) have no mass, they are affected by gravitational fields because these fields around large masses cause the fabric of space to warp. This was proven when Einstein predicted that during a solar eclipse stars not normally visible—those that appear close to the brilliant light of our sun—would appear in a different position due to this warping. Distant galaxies that would normally not be visible to people on earth can be seen due to the effect called gravitational lensing. This is where light from a distant source passes around a large gravitational field generated by a galaxy or star cluster, thereby bending the light and magnifying it, making it visible to the observer (see Illustration #10).

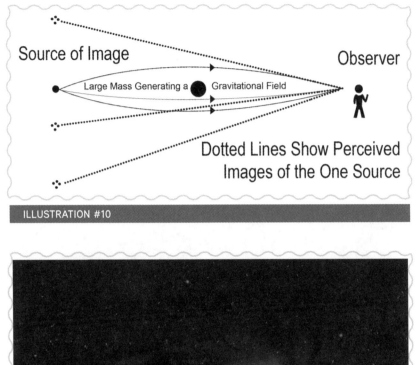

Source of Image

Observer

Large Mass Generating a ⬤ Gravitational Field

Dotted Lines Show Perceived
Images of the One Source

ILLUSTRATION #10

ILLUSTRATION #11

This artist's rendering shows an amazing example of gravitational lensing. Here you can see a quasar that has been calculated to be 10.4 billion light years from us with the lensing galaxy at a distance of 500 million light years. This famous image is called the Einstein Cross, where the bending light forms four images of the same quasar, in the shape of a cross. Is this just a coincidence or a sign in the heavens with a message from God saying "I AM"?

The way we experience time and space is not only affected by gravitational fields but also by the speed and direction that we are traveling relative to another point. As you approach the speed of light (the maximum speed limit of the universe), time for you slows down compared to another point. Space-time can be defined by the following illustration (see Illustration #12).

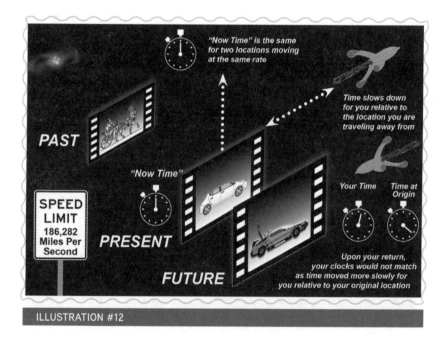

ILLUSTRATION #12

Imagine time and space as the frames of a film lined up one after another. Each frame represents a moment in time—past, present, and future. What is happening in the now is the same time frame in two different places when they are moving at the same rate together. Relative to each other these two locations seem to be at rest. However, when you move away from one of the locations, time is no longer the same. If you were on a spacecraft approaching the speed of light, time slows down for you relative to the location you are traveling away from. This reality has been proven in experiments where particles that decay at a certain rate are sped up close to the speed of light in a particle accelerator. When the particles are examined after the acceleration, the amount of decay that should have occurred has not happened. Time slowed down for the particles.

If you could exceed the speed of light, time would stop altogether for you. However, this is impossible due to the fact that as you accelerate your mass increases, requiring an increasing amount of energy to continue to accelerate. You would need an infinite amount of energy to reach that point, and that would infinitely increase your weight. So basically, you're stuck in this universe with the speed limit maxing out at about 186,282 miles per second.

The return trip from your ride in a spacecraft traveling at high speed would yield a fascinating phenomenon. When you arrive back at your original location, a significant amount of time would have passed at the original location compared to the time you experienced on your journey. Your clocks would be different even if they had been synchronized at the beginning of the trip. Ultimately, we can conclude that time is relative based on location, speed and direction, and gravitational fields. Space-time, which makes up the nature of our universe, has dimensions that are past, present, and future all existing together.

GOD IS OUTSIDE OF TIME

One thing is sure, God experiences time differently than we do. The Bible makes this clear when it says:

> *For a thousand years in Your sight are like yesterday when it is past, and like a watch in the night* (Psalm 90:4).

This reality is more than a metaphor, as God functions outside of time. From a physics point of view, a beam of light experiences time in a different time frame than we do. As it travels through space at its normative speed, all of time slows down to a moment, and in that timeless moment, from the photon's perspective, it can traverse the entire universe. What does this tell us about the true nature of time? Time, as we experience it, is not in reality what it seems and ultimately functions in a manner quite different from how we understand it. Hebrews 13:8 tells us, *"Jesus Christ is the same yesterday, today, and forever."*

Not only is Jesus pre-existent, He resides in a dimension where time is one continuous now. Perhaps His omnipresence is due to His ability to divide time into infinitesimal time frames (more on this in a moment). This would allow Him to visit us individually and relate to the billions of souls existing throughout time and space and so have the potential to be personally present for each of us. God's omniscience and foreknowledge of all events in time is due to God existing outside of time itself. Ultimately, the reality is that He knows every possible outcome of everyone's use of free will and consequently is able to forecast future events because from His perspective it has already occurred. John 16:13 indicates that this is the case for the Spirit of God:

> *However, when He, the Spirit of truth, has come, He will guide you into all truth; for He will not speak on His own authority, but whatever He hears He will speak; and He will tell you **things to come**.*

So we as believers in Messiah Jesus have the opportunity to connect with the Holy Spirit and have the benefit of tapping into the God who exists beyond time and space and hearing Him speak to us of "things to come." The Bible makes it clear that it is the normative function of life in relationship with the Shepherd to hear His voice, as it says in John 10:14-16:

> *I am the good shepherd; and I know My sheep, and am known by My own. As the Father knows Me, even so I know the Father; and I lay down My life for the sheep. And other sheep I have which are not of this fold; them also I must bring, and* **they will hear My voice.**

There is unimaginable benefit to drawing close to and being on the same frequency as the Creator of the universe. That is why I teach in my School of the Prophetic Harp that the most important thing that you can learn during our time on earth is to cultivate the ability to hear the voice of God. You can get familiar with His voice by getting into His Word and "*by reason of use, have* [your] *senses exercised*" (Heb. 5:14). By immersing yourself in the Bible, you tune in to His "still small voice" (see 1 Kings 19:12). You begin to increasingly recognize the tone of His words in those moments when He whispers into the ear of your mind.

I also recommend being intentional about spending time in private worship with Him, just sitting at His feet. My favorite places to do this are at the edge of my bed worshiping on my harp, in front of the fireplace with my Bible, or especially when driving in my car while on extended journeys. You can save yourself a world of grief if you take time to develop this in your life. Surely God always wants to give us His soft promptings for every decision of our lives both large and small. The key is to have a willing heart even if what He says is not necessarily what we want to hear. Be quick to listen and obey, having the same attitude as the boy Samuel who said *"Speak, for Your servant hears"* (1 Sam. 3:10).

As it is in the nature of God to know the beginning and end of all things, when we understand that He wants to let us in on His plan for our lives, He can guide us in our lives and so attain the highest measure of His blessing. Time is laid out for Him like a scroll that has already been written. In fact, Scripture teaches us that each one of us has a book in heaven that details our lives prior to the events taking place. It says in Psalm 139:16:

> *Your eyes saw my substance, being yet unformed. And in*
> *Your book they all were written, the days fashioned for me,*
> *when as yet there were none of them.*

In God's continuous now, such a document on our life and times is already published in the annals of heaven. This is possible because of the reality of how time as we experience it is an illusion. When comforting the family after the death of a lifelong friend, Einstein said that the death was of no consequence: "People like us, who believe in physics, know that the distinction between past, present, and future is only a stubbornly persistent illusion."

CHAPTER ELEVEN

HARPS, STRING THEORY, AND THE TOWER OF BABEL

A s previously stated, we know that the vibration of God's voice during creation was not a literal sound as defined by the audio spectrum that we can hear. More accurately, it was the unleashing of the resonance of God's will being imposed on the new reality of this dimension. All matter was called into existence and set vibrating with the essence of the energy that God put into the universe by His "voice." Also as mentioned, this initial infusion of energy into the universe is evident in the physics of matter as it relates to a concept called *mass defect*. This concept refers to the energy that was infused into the nucleus of every atom when it was first formed. It was as if God wound up the spring on a clock and set the whole universe "ticking."

Now let's consider the creation and nature of all matter in the universe. Currently, in the field of quantum physics, string theory is one of the most publicized theories of all that is. Simply stated, everything is comprised of filaments stretched out as strings vibrating with energy existing within a multiplicity of dimensions. Before anything existed, God used the vibration of His voice to create everything. He simply spoke and the whole universe began reverberating with the energy of His omnipotence. In a sense, like a well-tuned harp, every atom was created with an initial "tightening of the strings" when He wound up creation. Please note the humor in juxtaposing simple harp strings with a grand theory of everything. As a harpist I have a unique perspective on the subject matter of string theory.

So what is string theory? To break it down, we have to follow a string of thought (sorry for the pun). Matter is made up of molecules. Molecules are made up of the atoms found in the Periodic Table. Atoms are made up of electrons, protons, and neutrons. These fundamental particles have properties such as spin, charge, and mass and are defined by the arrangement of quarks that make them up. (Is this reminding you of the song "There's a Hole in the Bottom of the Sea"? You know how it goes: "There's a fleck on the speck on the tail on the frog on the bump on the branch on the log in the hole in the bottom of the sea.") Up to this point all this defining of matter is scientifically proven beyond any reasonable doubt. Now we come to the final speculation of what is in our quantum "Hole in the Bottom of the Sea." What could quarks possibly be made up of? String theory suggests that it's infinitesimally small (10^{-33} meters, which is considerably smaller than atoms themselves at 10^{-18} meters) strings vibrating with energy in an open and closed formation (see Illustration #13).

ILLUSTRATION #13

Strings that theoretically make up all matter vibrating with energy in an open and closed formation.

It is postulated that the properties of the matter formed by these filaments are determined by the manner and frequency of the vibration of these strings and the energy that is present. Strangely, this model cannot be defined mathematically in our ordinary three-dimensional space, but it requires no fewer than eleven dimensions for the math to work. However, when these dimensions are factored in, the math works elegantly and solves a number of issues that previous quantum theory was unable to address. The theory postulates that these extra dimensions are somehow tucked into each other, but, for us mere mortals, without the benefit of high-level math this concept is a bit above our pay grade. Wouldn't it be poetic if indeed all matter was ultimately comprised of tiny strings vibrating with energy just like a harp playing a cosmic song that held the universe together?

What string theory is attempting to do (amongst other objectives) is to take quantum field theory and bring it together with a model that explains the nature of gravity. Up till this point a full understanding of gravity has remained a mystery and has not been properly incorporated into a theory of "everything." The strange world of quantum physics has been able to accurately describe so much that is in our natural world and represents a marvelous achievement on the part of mankind.

THE TOWER OF BABEL REBORN

At this point in our discussion, as we consider man's highest level of technological achievement as represented in quantum physics, it brings to mind something incredible that God said about man in Genesis 11:5-6:

> But the Lord came down to see the city and the tower which the sons of men had built. And the Lord said, "Indeed the people are one and they all have one language, and this is what they begin to do; now **nothing that they propose to do will be withheld from them**.

In the context of this passage what is happening here is that mankind is attempting to build the Tower of Babel and their motive is questionable from God's perspective.

> And they said, "Come, let us build ourselves a city, and a tower whose top is in the heavens; let us make a name for ourselves, lest we be scattered abroad over the face of the whole earth" (Genesis 11:4).

Here, their actions reveal a deeply problematic issue in the condition of their hearts. Building this tower was really an act of defiance in the face of the Creator. Their motive was to build a city and a tower that reaches the heavens—independent of the Lord! They wanted to make a name for themselves and build a city where they would not be scattered over the earth, which was in direct violation of God's original intent for man to *"Be fruitful and multiply; fill the earth and subdue it"* (Gen. 1:28). Here is God's response:

> *"Come, let Us go down and there confuse their language, that they may not understand one another's speech." So the Lord scattered them abroad from there over the face of all the earth, and they ceased building the city. Therefore its name is called Babel, because there the Lord confused the language of all the earth; and from there the Lord scattered them abroad over the face of all the earth* (Genesis 11:7-9).

So it is that mankind is forced back into God's original plan to propagate and "fill" the world and man's arrogance is addressed. But what is fascinating about this whole narrative is the subterfuge that is evident behind it all. God is not known for exaggeration, and He says the consequences of their unity are that *"nothing that they propose to do will be withheld from them."* That's quite a statement coming from an all-knowing God. This suggests that God understood that, if left to themselves, man would quickly develop technology that would enable them to do *anything*—for better or for worse. This was all due to their ability to act and communicate as one unified network. Looking at our track record throughout history we can see that this is true, and the results have not proven to be the best.

In Daniel's magnificent prophecy of the end times we see an amazingly accurate description of today's world:

But you, Daniel, shut up the words, and seal the book until the time of the end; many shall run to and fro, and knowledge shall increase (Daniel 12:4).

It is clear that if God had not stepped in for our own good, we would have destroyed ourselves long ago. In Matthew 24:22, Jesus, speaking of the end times, actually states that in fact, unless those days are shortened all mankind will perish.

Humans, despite our strides in technological advancement, have not been the benevolent stewards of the planet as God intended. Our technologies, for all the marvels that they represent, have polluted our environment and caused death and destruction through an unbroken chain of war and conflict. It is ironic that with the unlocking of quantum physics and the creation of nuclear weapons of mass destruction, this very field of understanding has brought us to the brink of survival. It appears that without the ultimate intervention of the Lord we would get what we deserve—complete annihilation at our own hands.

Strangely, it is at the CERN particle accelerator facility that mankind's invention of the World Wide Web has in essence caused the Tower of Babel to be reborn. It appears as if man has finally caught up with himself and has created a work-around to address the confusion of languages. Our ability to unify and to talk one to another has accelerated technological advances. It is ominously prophetic that at the gates of the facility there is statue of Shiva, the Hindu god of destruction. With the onset of man's ability to be one with a common means of communication, can anything that we set our intellect to be withheld from us?

Despite this pessimistic outlook, it is important in our discussion to emphasize the need for mankind to find their way back to their Creator. Man can only find his best purpose by being in relationship with his Maker. This, however, is not the end of the story, and there is a bright hope for the future as will be expressed in the final chapter of this book.

CHAPTER TWELVE

GOD IS LIGHT: THE SCIENCE OF LIGHT

*This is the message which we have heard from Him and declare to you, that **God is light** and in Him is no darkness at all* (1 John 1:5).

The Bible states that "God is light," so there is something about the nature of light that tells us something about the nature of God. That is why a reasonable approach to understanding the mystery of God is to take the time to study the idea of light from a physics point of view. Scripture is abundant with references to light as it directly relates to the awesome nature of God. First Timothy 6:16 tells us, in the context of who Jesus is, that God dwells in unapproachable light:

Who alone has immortality, dwelling in unapproachable light, whom no man has seen or can see, to whom be honor and everlasting power. Amen.

The psalmist states:

Who cover Yourself with light as with a garment, who stretch out the heavens like a curtain (Psalm 104:2).

Here, God is described as being clothed with light and is the one who stretched out the heavens like a curtain. It is obvious that there is a connection between the very nature of God as Creator and His association with light that constantly surrounds Him. Light is a fundamental aspect of the universe and is an underlying component in Einstein's equation $E=mc^2$ ("c" being the speed of light), which we have frequently referred to in our discussion of quantum physics. The energy/mass equivalence tells us that the energy that went into the creation of matter initially involved an unfathomable burst of light as God spoke, "Let there be light." Scripture's divine inspiration is corroborated as there is no way that Moses, as he conveyed to us the Book of Genesis, could have possibly understood the profound accuracy of this statement as it related to the quantum reality of light as the main feature of the Big Bang.

It is no wonder that God, the originator of all matter, would be, by His very nature, one who dwells in unapproachable light. He is unapproachable, not just because He is holy and we as sinful man cannot coexist in the same location. From a physics point of view, the awesome glory of the kind of being who wields the force of energy that brought the entire cosmos into existence is simply inaccessible to our frail flesh-and-blood bodies. Herein lies a mystery that further gives us a sense of awe and wonder. This same God, who simply can't be approached due to the very nature of His being, desires above all things for us to come near to Him. But how could this be possible?

Despite that fact that God is unapproachable, we see an amazing moment in the history of mankind in Exodus 24, and this is repeated in similar scenes found in Ezekiel and Revelation. We will look more deeply into the physics that surround the throne of God in the following chapter where we discuss the God dimension. For now, we see the awesome God, Creator of the cosmos, having a meal with a select group of humans—who in this case did not perish in His presence.

> *Then Moses went up, also Aaron, Nadab, and Abihu, and seventy of the elders of Israel, and they saw the God of Israel. And there was under His feet as it were a paved work of sapphire stone, and it was like the very heavens in its clarity. But on the nobles of the children of Israel He did not lay His hand. So they saw God, and they ate and drank* (Exodus 24:9-11).

It is apparent that the elders of Israel had a special invitation to dinner that allowed them to see the God of Israel, at least at a distance. God must have somehow shielded them from the full impact of His radiance. So it appears that it is possible for man to encounter the living God, but with special conditions and considerations in place. This brings to mind the face-to-face experience that Moses had in Exodus 3 where the God of light spoke through a source of light in the form of a burning bush:

> *And the Angel of the Lord appeared to him in a flame of fire from the midst of a bush. So he looked, and behold, the bush was burning with fire, but the bush was not*

consumed. Then Moses said, "I will now turn aside and see this great sight, why the bush does not burn."

So when the Lord saw that he turned aside to look, God called to him from the midst of the bush and said, "Moses, Moses!"

And he said, "Here I am."

Then He said, "Do not draw near this place. Take your sandals off your feet, for the place where you stand is holy ground." Moreover He said, "I am the God of your father—the God of Abraham, the God of Isaac, and the God of Jacob." And Moses hid his face, for he was afraid to look upon God (Exodus 3:2-6).

It is during this awesome encounter that God reveals to Moses the name that is to be known as *"My name forever, and this is My memorial to all generations"* (Exod. 3:15). In verse 14 we read, *"And God said to Moses, 'I AM WHO I AM.'"*

God warns Moses to keep his distance and remove his sandals due to the holiness of the ground he is standing on. From a physics point of view, today's technology allows for sound to be conveyed through the use of a "plasma speaker" where an excited state of energy modulates the air around the plasma field between two electrodes. In this kind of setup, high fidelity sound in the spectrum of our hearing, as well as frequencies beyond our range of hearing, can be transmitted into a room. Could it be that God chose to use this burning bush as a plasma field to convey the vibration of His voice? Regardless, as the bush was not consumed there was certainly a frequency of the supernatural in operation that day. It is interesting to note that God chose light as the means by which He first spoke to Moses, the most significant transcriber of God's Word—the Bible.

Perhaps Moses needed to remove his sandals to be properly grounded to preserve his safety in the energy field of God's presence. This may also be the case if we consider the nature of the Ark of the Covenant. This amazing gold box represented the very presence of God on earth. In more than one instance we see the consequences of not taking seriously the holiness of this sacred object (see 1 Sam. 5 and 6). The study of the Ark is a fascinating topic beyond the scope of this book. However, it is interesting to note that there seems to be a field of energy that breaks out on those who do not handle the Ark as prescribed by the Law of Moses—whether this is due to a law of physics, a judgement from God, or a bit of both.

As we return to the subject at hand, we can conclude that the qualities of light reflect the nature of God. We have just discussed the correlation between God's creative powers and the energy expressed as light. This book has also already spoken in detail about photons traveling for billions of years to reach us from distant galaxies at the "speed of light" but experiencing only a moment of time relative to our time frame. We can also conclude that as light is an aspect of God's nature, He intended for us to come to understand that He too is beyond time and His frame of reference is different from us who are time bound. So, not only is God omnipotent and the origina-tor of limitless energy, but He also is omniscient, being the Master of time and space.

John 1:4-5 speaks of the life giving quality of light.

> *In Him was life, and the life was the light of men. And the light shines in the darkness, and the darkness did not comprehend it.*

The manner in which life-giving energy is transmitted through the fusion nuclear reaction in our sun is something we take for granted. The earth receives this seemingly limitless source of warmth and light at just the right distance from the sun in the "Goldilocks Zone" at 93 million miles away. The radiant energy is perfectly distributed by our atmosphere shielding us from harmful radiation and is regulated by the exacting tilt of the earth of 23.5 degrees, giving us our seasons and seed time and harvest. The conversion of this energy efficiently generates the cycle of rain that waters our lands and makes food production possible for our populations. This conversion of the sun's energy into food energy is by the design of the God of light who uses the light of His creation to give life to all of us. How appropriate it is to describe God as the light of men. Sadly, not all accept this light and choose to live in the darkness. This includes the demonic hosts who constantly work toward the detriment of mankind.

So, the truth remains. God is light, and is not the author of evil. When mankind rejects the light, he is left to his own devices and suffers the consequences of his own folly. God's light continues to shine in the darkness like a lighthouse that guides the souls of men safely into the harbor of His love.

The last chapter in this book will deal with the cosmology and theology of the end of the age, but in the context of our discussion of light we see that God is ultimately the source of light in the end of all things. Revelation 22:5 tells us:

> *There shall be no night there: They need no lamp nor light*
> *of the sun, for the Lord God gives them light. And they*
> *shall reign forever and ever.*

In this verse we can see that from the beginning, where the light of God was first released, to the very end, where the Lord Himself is the source of light even as our sun sustains us with its life-giving light, we will bask in the light of His goodness forever. Here we also see the bright hope of the ultimate, intended destiny of those who have surrendered to this light. Alongside God, *"they shall reign forever and ever."* Where there previously was a chasm between mankind and the Lord of light, those lost in darkness can see a great light as Isaiah 9:2 promises:

> *The people who walked in darkness have seen a great light.*

Ultimately, we who have accepted this light have an awesome destiny, not just in the future when the Kingdom of God is fully established on earth, but even now we have a role to play in the proclamation of His excellency! First Peter 2:9 tells us:

> *But you are a chosen race, a royal priesthood, a holy nation,*
> *a people for his own possession, that you may proclaim the*
> *excellencies of him who called you out of darkness into his*
> *marvelous light* (ESV).

We have the wonderful opportunity to step out of the dark and come into the light. The way we can come to this formerly unapproachable light is through the Light of the World, who gave His life for us so that He could bridge the darkness for us as John 1:12 promises:

> *But as many as received Him, to them He gave the right to*
> *become children of God, to those who believe in His name.*

It is now possible to come to His light, but we must be transformed in order for us to be able to come near to Him. We end up as the sons and daughters of light and are transformed into His likeness. First Thessalonians 5:5 exhorts us:

You are all children of light, children of the day. We are not of the night or of the darkness (ESV).

First Corinthians 15:52 speaks of this final transformation:

In a moment, in the twinkling of an eye, at the last trump: for the trumpet shall sound, and the dead shall be raised incorruptible, and we shall be changed (KJV).

This final transformation will give us a glorified body that will have the capacity not only to live forever but to be able to endure the unimaginable and wonderful glory of the Lord of light.

First Corinthians 15:53-57 gloriously concludes:

For this corruptible must put on incorruption, and this mortal must put on immortality. So when this corruptible has put on incorruption, and this mortal has put on immortality, then shall be brought to pass the saying that is written: "Death is swallowed up in victory." "O Death, where is your sting? O Hades, where is your victory?" The sting of death is sin, and the strength of sin is the law. But thanks be to God, who gives us the victory through our Lord Jesus Christ.

CHAPTER THIRTEEN

THE GOD DIMENSION AND THE FREQUENCY OF HEAVEN

As we enter into our discussion of the God dimension and the frequency of heaven we begin to see the lines blur between the physics of our natural world and the mystery of the heavenly realms. The concept of a "dimension" in physics all boils down to where something is and how to mathematically describe that location. We live in a three-dimensional world that that can be defined by width, depth, and height with the added dimension of time. So we can conceptualize the first three dimensions intuitively; however, when it comes to our perception of time it is much harder to wrap our heads around the idea that time is relative. Regardless of whether we intellectually can grasp this concept, it does not change the fact that it is a reality. Hopefully, as you have read this book your understanding of the reality of time has expanded and the spiritual significance of this is taking shape in your mind.

In quantum physics, string theory relies on the idea that there are multiple dimensions beyond the four that we just mentioned. However, at this point there is no way of testing the premise, so one could say you'll have to take it by faith. Many credible scientists are spending their life's energies believing that such a concept could be a reality. Multiple dimensions suggest that wrapped up in our dimension are other dimensions that, in a sense, are occupying the same time and space only at this point they are unobservable. String theory suggests that one-dimensional strings vibrate with energy and interact across these multiple dimensions forming *branes*. The concept attempts to explain how these branes and the strings themselves define the properties of matter and particularly of how gravity itself functions.

This all sounds similar to our understanding of the spiritual realm as contained in the Scriptures. In Second Corinthians 12:2, Paul the apostle recounts an amazing experience that he had when he encountered a heavenly dimension:

> *I know a man in Christ who fourteen years ago—whether in the body I do not know, or whether out of the body I do not know, God knows—such a one was caught up to the third heaven.*

When Paul speaks of the "third heaven" this implies a first and a second, although they are not explicitly mentioned in the Scriptures. The first heaven refers to the "troposphere," which is the lowest layer of Earth's atmosphere varying in depth from an average of 12 miles over the tropical regions to as low as 4.3 miles over the North and South Poles during winter. Just beyond that, the second heaven corresponds to the celestial realm where the moon and the stars are viewed. Finally, we arrive at the God dimension, the "highest heavens" in Deuteronomy 10:14:

> *Indeed heaven and the highest heavens belong to the Lord your God, also the earth with all that is in it.*

In Matthew 6:9 Jesus clearly identifies the dimension God resides in when He instructed us to pray *"Our Father in heaven."* Where exactly is this dimension? Could one get in a spaceship and fly there? Scripture seems to indicate that this "God dimension" is a heavenly dimension that is superimposed right here in our midst. Matthew exclusively uses the term the *Kingdom of Heaven,* but in most cases the term is interchangeable with the *Kingdom of God* in the other Gospels. Some Bible teachers interpret these two terms as having a significant difference in meaning, but when comparing the Gospels the term is in most cases synonymous. Matthew 4:17 tells us:

> *From that time Jesus began to preach and to say, "Repent, for the kingdom of heaven is at hand."*

Jesus also said in Luke 17:21:

> *Nor will people say, "Here it is," or "There it is," because the kingdom of God is in your midst* (NIV).

Could it be that this implies more than just the imminent revelation of the Kingdom of Heaven? Is God's dominion extended beyond heaven and in some way in our midst? I suggest that the actual workings of the Kingdom of Heaven overlap into our dimension in the same way multiple dimensions are inherent to string theory. Again, in Matthew 6:10 we read:

> *Your kingdom come. Your will be done on earth as it is in heaven.*

God's will can be superimposed on earth in a manner that is consistent with heaven itself. Jesus would not have given us these instructions for prayer if He did not intend for the answer to be not just possible but a reality. Here, we have the great hope that even in this time frame, through our partnership of intercession in concert with His will, the Kingdom of Heaven can come to this dimension. This is the essence of effectual prayer—with the intention of our faith we tune in to the frequency of faith that is synchronized with heaven. We resonate with the plans and purposes already in the heart of God, and we become the receiver of that impulse from the Creator. On this side of heaven, that which is "as it is in heaven" can be transmitted to earth. Jesus consistently modeled this for us in His own prayer life and consequently was always tuned to the frequency of His Father. Wonderfully, we can emulate this too. All we must do is draw close enough to the Father to hear His still small voice and do only what we "see" the Father doing on this earthly plane. That is why we must cultivate a lifestyle that intentionally focuses on tuning in to the frequency of heaven.

If you have a revelation of what is happening in the God dimension and understand the nature of the frequency of heaven that permeates that rarified atmosphere, you can be transformed here in our dimension. You can tap into that frequency and be an influence on this worldly plane as you are energized by the Spirit of the God of light.

Let's take a glimpse into the heavenly realm and see the glory that can transform us and empower us to be a conduit of the frequency of heaven. Hebrews 9:24 tells us:

> *For Christ has not entered the holy places made with hands, which are copies of the true, but into heaven itself, now to appear in the presence of God for us.*

Notice the intercessory role that Jesus plays on our behalf. Jesus acts as the High Priest of our faith, and on a quantum level His mastery of time and space makes it possible for Him to be simultaneously attentive to billions of prayers at a given moment. He sees you and your heart's cry individually and personally.

The holy places mentioned in Hebrews 9:24 refer to the places in the Tabernacle of Moses and Solomon's Temple that housed the Ark of the Covenant. As magnificent as they were, they are only a shadow compared to the actual reality of heaven. In a vivid picture of the God dimension we see a description of the brightness of the God who is clothed in a wild array of frequencies of light:

> *And above the firmament over their heads was the likeness of a throne, in appearance like a sapphire stone; on the likeness of the throne was a likeness with the appearance of a man high above it. Also from the appearance of His waist and upward I saw, as it were, the color of amber with the appearance of fire all around within it; and from the appearance of His waist and downward I saw, as it were, the appearance of fire with brightness all around. Like the appearance of a rainbow in a cloud on a rainy day, so was the appearance of the brightness all around it.*

> *This was the appearance of the likeness of the glory of the*
> *Lord* (Ezekiel 1:26-28).

This glimpse into the throne room of the King of the universe speaks of the glory of the Lord. However, it leads us to think about what the physics of heaven must incorporate as far as energy and light are concerned. Again, light is a key feature of what clearly is the center of power in the cosmos, and at that center is a Man on a throne. His name is Jesus. Note the presence of a rainbow in proximity to the throne—we will see this in the scene from Revelation. In Revelation 4:2-5, we see the similarities in Ezekiel's description of this apex of power; however, there is a progression of revelation as we see more detail.

> *Immediately I was in the Spirit; and behold, a throne set*
> *in heaven, and One sat on the throne. And He who sat*
> *there was like a jasper and a sardius stone in appearance;*
> *and there was a rainbow around the throne, in appear-*
> *ance like an emerald. Around the throne were twenty-*
> *four thrones, and on the thrones I saw twenty-four elders*
> *sitting, clothed in white robes; and they had crowns of gold*
> *on their heads. And from the throne proceeded lightnings,*
> *thunderings, and voices.*

We notice in both Ezekiel and in Revelation the presence of a rainbow. In fact, John identifies that the rainbow, more specifically, has the color of emerald. What does this signify about the physics of heaven? What would precipitate an emerald rainbow? What might this shade of green mean?

On earth we witness the seven bands of rainbow color that are due to a refraction of light through raindrops. The visible frequencies of light from our star, the sun, are split into the familiar range of colors and the "spectrometry" that is displayed can be used to determine its chemical composition as is the case with any star. It is interesting to note that spectroscopic studies were a key part of the development of quantum physics, including experimentation relating to Max Planck's blackbody radiation, Einstein's photoelectric effect, and Niels Bohr's atomic structure model. Could we also extend our own spectral analysis on this phenomenon of the green rainbow and conclude something about the frequency of heaven?

Let's consider the color green. Green happens to be the center band of color and frequency in the rainbow. Green is the color on earth that suggests life. The High Priest in the days of Moses' Tabernacle and Solomon's Temple wore a breastplate studded with twelve stones, each representing one of the twelve tribes of Israel. The green emerald gemstone on this High Priest's *ephod* may suggest the answer to meaning of this color. The emerald gemstone represents the tribe of Judah, which from the Hebrew יְהוּדָה (Yehudah) means it is the "praise tribe." Praise that surrounds the throne of God sets up a harmonious vibration of heavenly sound. Perhaps that is what is generating the frequencies that manifest as an emerald rainbow that correspondingly encircles the throne of the Lord. We will discuss this more thoroughly in the next chapter.

In John's depiction of this awesome scene from around the throne of heaven, we see that there "proceeded lightnings, thunderings, and voices." Lightning and thunder imply that there are powerful electromagnetic fields present. This is logically to be expected in the presence of the God who created all the energy in the universe. It is awe inspiring and comforting to consider that this place of power is where we draw all our sustenance, as the Scriptures encourage us in Philippians 4:19:

*And my God shall supply all your need according to His
riches in glory by Christ Jesus.*

In addition to this amazing array of colors and energy that fills the
God dimension there is a manifestation of sound. This feature of the
frequency of heaven requires special attention and will be addressed
in the following chapter. What is this sound? Revelation 15:2 tells us:

*And I saw something like a sea of glass mingled with fire,
and those who have the victory over the beast, over his
image and over his mark and over the number of his name,
standing on the sea of glass, having* **harps of God**.

The sound is music—harp music.

CHAPTER FOURTEEN

QUANTUM MUSIC AND THE SOUND OF HEAVEN

Music is a language that is universally understood. The physics of music demonstrate that a set ratio of frequencies mathematically display the pleasing nature of harmonies (see Chapter Eighteen for a more expanded description of this concept). It seems that God has purposefully entrenched into the fabric of the universe the tonal sequence of the musical scale and we, as His creation, have an appreciation of this sonic quality. There are seven steps in this scale, and it reflects the anomaly of the number seven found in the colors of the rainbow and in the seven days of creation. The number seven keeps popping up throughout the Bible, but this is the topic of another study.

Even in the secular world, music is understood to have healing properties. Therapeutic musicians, particularly harpists, are employed to play for patients in post-operative situations. Studies have shown that patients have on average a 25 percent improved outcome when given the benefit of having a harpist play while recovering from surgical procedures. So, how much more does the playing of an anointed musician bring the power of God to the cells of the bodies of those who need healing?

So what is quantum music? To fully appreciate the significance of the power of music on a quantum level, we must revisit the throne room in the God dimension. Revelation 14:2 describes the musical atmosphere around God's throne permeating it with the very frequencies of heaven:

> And I heard a voice from heaven, like the voice of many waters, and like the voice of loud thunder. And I heard the sound of harpists playing their harps.

Here, we hear the voice from heaven, which sounded like many waters and loud thunder. I have had the privilege of visiting Niagara Falls as it is not too far from my home in Ontario, Canada. (Be sure to experience this at least once in your life; I suggest the magnificent view from the Canadian side.) The falls are truly inspiring, but what is awesome, apart from the visual aspect of the sheer volume of water pouring over the edge, is the roar of the sound of the waters cascading downward. This sound is what I think of when I consider this description of the voice of many waters from Revelation 14. The voice of loud thunder is an appropriate comparison for the sound of Niagara Falls.

It is intriguing that this sound, often described as "white noise," is relaxing and people often use it to help them sleep or to block out unwanted sound. In my high school electronics class, each student built a stereo amplifier with the option of incorporating a "pink noise" generator to help equalize and balance the overall sound tone in a given room. You can find samples of such generators on the Internet and listen to options of "pink," "white," and "brown," each with their variation of tones that represent the full range of the spectrum of sound. Each variation sounds like the waters of a waterfall or rain pouring down. There must be something about the simultaneous generation of all tones across the audio spectrum (typically 20 hertz to 20,000 hertz) that resonates with our being. However, I believe that this sound is connected with a symphony of worship that makes up the soundscape of heaven.

What is remarkable about the music of heaven, especially in light of the fact that I frequently give instruction to harp students at my Schools of the Prophetic Harp, is this reference to the playing of harps in heaven. Despite my bias toward encouraging the playing of the harp for worship, intercession, healing, deliverance, and the prophetic, this most remarkable sound stands out as more than a cliché. Even though it is stereotypical to envision harpists playing harps in heaven, I'm sure that in heaven more than one type of instrument will be played. However, it should be noted that other than the harp, the only other instrument that is mentioned in the book of Revelation is the trumpet used in proclamations. In my harp schools, where I have had as many as 33 students in a room, one of the first things that I teach is how to tune the harps to a scale that is called a pentatonic scale. The quality of this scale is that regardless of the number harpists playing notes simultaneously the overall sound of the group is harmonious. Envision, if you can, a room full of harpists worshiping on their instrument with all their heart, in perfect harmony at all times. It is a glorious experience. I am privileged to have a role in helping to restore this sound of worship as it was in the days of King David in his tabernacle. Imagine now, in the highest heavens, a myriad of harp worshipers creating an atmosphere that fills the God dimension with music. Now that would be something worth exporting to earth and that, in part, is what we are attempting to recreate in my harp schools around the world.

The power of the quantum reality of music is tied in to the frequency of heaven, which is overwhelmingly expressed through worship with music. We have discussed how on a quantum level our intention affects both the natural and spiritual realms. The highest level of the release of the frequency of heaven is found in worship, as worship is the intentional act of adoration of the Creator. In this expression of love, regardless of whether worship is played on the harp or some other instrument or even simply our voices, there is something supernatural that occurs through the deliberate nature of this act.

Psalm 22:3 in the World English Bible translates the phrase, "*But you are holy, you who inhabit the praises of Israel.*" When we worship and praise the God of heaven, something supernatural takes place. God inhabits our praise. Again, our intent in worship invites the God of the universe to present Himself in such a way that He actually expresses Himself through it. When we gather in His name, He has promised that He will be present. Matthew 18:19-20 corroborates this when Jesus promises:

> *Again I say to you that if two of you agree on earth concerning anything that they ask, it will be done for them by My Father in heaven. For where two or three are gathered together in My name, I am there in the midst of them.*

What a wonderful promise. The difference between just going for coffee and experiencing the presence of God is our intent to gather together in His name! Last time I checked, wherever the presence of God is, amazing things take place. It is interesting to note that the word used in this passage for "agree" is the Greek word *sumphoneo* (Strong's #G4856). It brings to mind the idea that as we are in agreement and in unity of our intent, we are like a symphony orchestra that is in harmony with each other like a concert of praise! In that place of unity our requests are granted by our Father in heaven.

So the difference between just the playing of music and actually evoking the presence of God is our intent on a quantum level. Therefore, not only is the universe affected around us as we worship, the God who created the universe enters our dimension and brings the frequency of the supernatural.

As a harpist, I have a unique perspective on all things that relate to harps in the Bible. When you do a study on the word *harp* in your concordance, you will see a surprising number of references. It seems that this instrument is God's favorite. There is a whole rich vein of truth that stems from the role of the harp, particularly in the life of King David and his tabernacle that is being restored in our day. This is the subject of another book of mine entitled *As It Is in Heaven*. However, in our discussion of the quantum realities of music there is one further concept related to the harp that should be mentioned.

Returning to the book of Revelation, we see a remarkable paradigm that is astounding:

> *Now when He had taken the scroll, the four living creatures and the twenty-four elders fell down before the Lamb, each having a harp, and golden bowls full of incense, which are the prayers of the saints* (Revelation 5:8).

A great mystery is revealed in this passage and would be easy to pass over if we did not think carefully and clearly about it. Let's consider what is happening here. The 24 elders, who are surely majestic individuals with a remarkable task, are, of all things, harpists and they are in close proximity to the very throne of God. Their task is more than just playing their harps in worship. If we read this at face value, it is here that our prayers are presented in heaven in the form of incense. It seems to indicate that when we pray something actually materializes in heaven and appears in the golden bowls.

Incidentally, it is from this portion of Scripture that the phrase "harp and bowl worship and prayer" is derived. This concept involves the use of music and Scriptures to spontaneously be used in intercession and has been popularized in places like the International House of Prayer in Kansas City and houses of prayer around the world. For a number of years I held Schools of the Prophetic Harp on the top of the Mount of Olives in Jerusalem at the Jerusalem House of Prayer for All Nations. I instructed their staff in the use of the harp for intercession, and the harp is now their primary instrument that is used in their 24/7 prayer sets. So as we see 24/7 houses of prayer using the "harp and bowl" mode of intercession mainly using guitars and keyboards, I hope to see actual harps being used more and more!

Incense typically is some kind of particulate that carries the beautiful scent of the material it is made from, and it is released into the air as it is burned. Somehow, on a quantum level, the words that we speak in prayer (especially if we sing our prayers accompanied by musical instruments such as a harp) cross the dimensions of time and space and take physical form in heaven. This is clearly indicated in this scripture and it is not a metaphor or poetic language. When the prayer appears in the golden bowls it actually is a substance that exists in that dimension and changes the atmosphere around the throne of God. But what is really significant is that this whole process is accompanied by the sound of the harp.

I believe that it is the sonic quality of the harp and its simplicity of design that makes it the instrument of choice for the music of heaven. The gentle voice of the harp speaks of the need to quiet oneself in order to hear the beautiful melody, just as we must quiet our hearts to hear the still, quiet small voice of God. The specific roll of harp worship in conveying our prayers to the throne of God is profound. The strings of the harp are stretched out over a frame of varying lengths and corresponding frequencies. Like the strings in string theory, they vibrate and something tangible is the result—our prayers are answered here on this earthly plane. This is all accomplished while being accompanied by the sound of harp strings being played by the 24 elders. One can't help but conclude that something is happening in the quantum realm where matter and energy is being affected as these heavenly vibrations and frequencies are being generated by our prayers. This is a clear manifestation of the frequency of the supernatural.

Revelation 8:3-5 gives us a dramatic picture of what happens with the incense of prayer as it re-enters our dimension:

> *Then another angel, having a golden censer, came and stood at the altar. He was given much incense, that he should offer it with the prayers of all the saints upon the golden altar which was before the throne. And the smoke of the incense, with the prayers of the saints, ascended before God from the angel's hand. Then the angel took the censer, filled it with fire from the altar, and threw it to the earth. And there were noises, thunderings, lightnings, and an earthquake.*

Many religions use incense in their prayer rituals, but it is a counterfeit of the reality that is the manifestation in heaven of true prayer. Like the Ark of the Covenant in the earthly holy places, they are a shadow of the reality of the incense that is manifested in heaven when prayer that is based in the truth of God's Word is offered to

God. This is why when I am worshiping on the harp I do not like to have any kind of artificial scent in the room. On a number of occasions, the sweet fragrance of heaven has manifested during worship, and I would never want a man-made smell to interfere with experiencing the real incense of heaven as it crosses over from the God dimension.

It is clear in this passage from Revelation 8 that the incense that was generated through the prayers of the saints is used by the angel in a powerful response that is literally thrown to the earth. One of my favorite works of fiction is by Frank Peretti in his books *This Present Darkness* and *Piercing the Darkness*. In these books he graphically portrays how the angelic host relies on the prayers of the saints before they are able to move on behalf of the Kingdom of God. I believe this portrayal is accurate as we see in this portion of Scripture how the incense ascended before God from the angel's hand. Our prayers reach the throne of God in a literal fashion. Our prayer lives will be changed dynamically when we get a hold of the revelation of this reality. We can know that our prayers will be answered with a certainty when we embrace this reality. This is affirmed First John 5:15:

> *And if we know that He hears us, whatever we ask, we know that we have the petitions that we have asked of Him.*

This is even more emphatically expressed in the Amplified Version:

> *And if we know [for a fact, as indeed we do] that He hears and listens to us in whatever we ask, we [also] know [with settled and absolute knowledge] that we have [granted to us] the requests which we have asked from Him.*

The result of the angel being empowered with the ammunition of prayer was that when it was thrown down to earth *"there were noises, thunderings, lightnings, and an earthquake."* Something dramatic on earth took place as the result of pouring out the incense from the prayers that had been gathered in the censer and hurled down like a stone in a slingshot. We can have confidence that as we are tuned in to the frequency of the supernatural, our prayers will shake the earth.

So let's connect the dots. Playing the harp (or any other instrument, including our voices) sets up a harmonious vibration that, when played as worship or intercession, carries the very presence of God. The fact is, our prayers are ushered into God's presence with the sound of the harp via the golden bowls of the 24 elders around God's throne. This is comparable to how our radios receive AM/FM waves at certain preset frequencies. Interestingly, a radio signal often uses what is called a "carrier frequency" to deliver the signal to our radios. So it appears that specifically *harp worship* is the medium by which our prayers are conveyed to God. Part of this beautiful mystery is the opportunity for us to reciprocate heaven with our worship, even with the playing of the harp here on earth. It is like a high-speed Internet connection to heaven, especially when we are using the same equipment on either side of our respective dimensions. Harp playing really is just an example of simply releasing a sonic vibration that is an expression of the intention of our faith.

We can also operate in the frequency of the supernatural when we speak words of faith that are in line with the heart of God, but doing so with the use of music is a powerful mechanism modeled in heaven. Scripture admonishes us to use music as a tool for enhancing our spiritual lives, as it says in Colossians 3:16:

Let the word of Christ dwell in you richly in all wisdom, teaching and admonishing one another in psalms and hymns and spiritual songs, singing with grace in your hearts to the Lord.

Regardless of the specific manner in which we express our faith, it has an effect on this earthly plane on a quantum level. Hebrews 11:1-3 tells us that our faith literally is the substance that is the evidence of the unseen that manifests in the material realm.

Now faith is the substance of things hoped for, the evidence of things not seen. For by it the elders obtained a good testimony.

By faith we understand that the worlds were framed by the word of God, so that the things which are seen were not made of things which are visible.

As God's children with the same spiritual DNA, He wants us to speak words of faith that bring into existence a manifestation of His plans and purposes on earth. Ultimately, when we bring to bear our expression of faith, particularly expressed in a manner that causes a sonic vibration through music or voice, we set up a resonance that reverberates in both heaven and earth. This resonance causes an effect that can be defined as the frequency of the supernatural.

CHAPTER FIFTEEN

Spiritual Warfare, the Sound of Deliverance, and God's Secret End-Time Weapon

In recent years, the topic of spiritual warfare has been addressed by numerous publications that are worthy of our attention. However, my approach to this area of truth is from the particular perspective of a musician, psalmist, and prophetic harpist in the mode of King David. The subject matter of this book has also examined the realities of how the spiritual world relates to that of quantum physics, but it is difficult to use hard science to describe what is taking place behind the scenes in the spiritual dimensions. There are, however, parallels that the natural realm gives us that suggest what may be going on in the supernatural dimension. Just because the scientific methodology cannot be applied to every phenomenon we encounter does not mean that it is any less real. Despite the inability to define this topic through scientific experimentation, I will share a few incidents from personal experience that will help validate what is clearly expressed in Scripture. This reality relates to the conflict that is actively taking place all around us that originates in a dimension outside of our natural understanding. A foundational scripture that is commonly quoted in this regard is Ephesians 6:12:

> *For we do not wrestle against flesh and blood, but against principalities, against powers, against the rulers of the darkness of this age, against spiritual hosts of wickedness in the heavenly places.*

These demonic principalities and powers operating from a heavenly dimension outside our own seek to extend their control of the world around us to the detriment of all mankind. We will now address a unique approach to dealing with their rulership, which will help to overturn their influence in the material world and in your personal life.

From the previous chapter we acknowledged that God-directed music sets up a vibration, not only in the air around us but with a resonance that reaches the heavenly places. I propose that this Spirit-charged vibration of worship runs a kind of interference pattern that disarms the rulers of darkness. So as we address this subject, we will see that indeed our use of worshipful music generates a frequency of the supernatural that has a dramatic effect as it relates to this spiritual warfare.

Second Chronicles 20:20-23 is an outstanding example that highlights the use of prophetically directed worship music that overturned a dire situation:

So they rose early in the morning and went out into the Wilderness of Tekoa; and as they went out, Jehoshaphat stood and said, "Hear me, O Judah and you inhabitants of Jerusalem: Believe in the Lord your God, and you shall be established; believe His prophets, and you shall prosper." And when he had consulted with the people, he appointed those who should sing to the Lord, and who should praise the beauty of holiness, as they went out before the army and were saying:

"Praise the Lord, for His mercy endures forever."

Now when they began to sing and to praise, the Lord set ambushes against the people of Ammon, Moab, and Mount Seir, who had come against Judah; and they were defeated. For the people of Ammon and Moab stood up against the inhabitants of Mount Seir to utterly kill and destroy them. And when they had made an end of the inhabitants of Seir, they helped to destroy one another.

In this incident, Israel was beset with a deadly enemy confronting them in the natural realm. No doubt the demonic forces intent on their destruction were set against them behind the scenes in the heavenly dimension. In this situation, a prophetic word came directing Israel to put the musicians at the front of the army to sing to the Lord and praise the beauty of holiness. This hardly seems like a viable defense against a foe that is arrayed against them. However, we see that the end result was the enemy literally killed themselves in a wave of confusion and self-destruction. Believe it or not, this power is still available to those who are prepared to wage spiritual warfare when prophetically directed by the Lord of hosts.

SPIRITUAL WARFARE ON THE WALLS OF JERUSALEM

Here is an account of an amazing moment that took place with the prophetic harp team I assembled for the 2015 blood moon event that I spoke of at the beginning of this book. I believe that this incident is a modern-day example of the power of music in intercession and spiritual warfare, which I have personally experienced.

The book of Nehemiah tells of the dedication of the walls of Jerusalem after they had been rebuilt:

> *Now at the dedication of the wall of Jerusalem they sought out the Levites in all their places, to bring them to Jerusalem to celebrate the dedication with gladness, both with thanksgivings and singing, with cymbals and stringed instruments and harps* (Nehemiah 12:27).

Here we see an ancient event commemorating the rebuilding of the walls of Jerusalem after the return of the Jews from the Babylonian captivity. Nehemiah 12:38-40 describes two teams of harpists proceeding on the walls that converged at the temple site as they dedicated the walls to the Lord. We as a team of harpists sought to recreate this event as we mounted the walls of present-day Jerusalem in 2015.

Here was our strategy. Our team of harpists had been trained in "harp warfare" in previous Schools of the Prophetic Harp that I had held in Jerusalem over the years. So this team (I called them my "A Team") was ready for battle. We ascended the walls at the entry point at the Jaffa Gate with one team heading toward the Zion Gate and the other in the opposite direction toward the Lions' Gate. The plan was for the harpists to walk along the wall singing and worshiping on the harp and to distribute a set of harpists to pray and intercede over the Old City of Jerusalem, one set at each gate. We would converge at the Golden Gate, the gate where one day Messiah will enter once again and take up the throne of Israel! We were to synchronize a specific time when our harp worship team was to sing a song of peace and protection over the city as commanded in the Scriptures:

> *Pray for the peace of Jerusalem: "May they prosper who love you"* (Psalm 122:6).

Just as the teams were deployed, on my way to the Golden Gate I descended the walls at Herod's Gate leaving a final team of harpists there as the access further toward the Lions' Gate had been blocked off. I rounded the northeast corner of the walls when I heard an explosion. I quickly retraced my steps to look down the street back towards Herod's Gate in the Muslim Quarter and saw a plume of smoke rising near the Damascus Gate. With sirens blaring in the background, I immediately picked up my cell phone to check in with the teams to ensure everyone was alright. All was well as we concluded our intercessory prayer and rallied at the Golden Gate. It was at that time that my team told me what they had experienced.

Apparently, the perpetrators of this explosion had set off a gasoline bomb across from the Damascus Gate just down from Herod's Gate. My final team that was set at that gate had something unusual happen at that point. To their amazement, in the confusion someone ran by the gate, took out a pistol, pulled out the clip, and threw the gun at the feet of our harpists and ran away. It appears that in their flight from the authorities, fear of capture had gripped them and the perpetrators fled the scene without doing any further harm to anyone. It was also reported that this same thing happened in a separate location at the same time.

I have since pondered what was happening in the spirit realm at the time of this event. What are the chances of this taking place while my team was in position worshiping and praying protection over the city of Jerusalem at the exact moment of this act of violence? What would have happened if intercession was not being offered to the Lord at that moment and what evil forces were restrained as a result of our musical prayer? We won't know for sure until we have an opportunity to have an "instant replay" of this moment when we arrive in heaven. However, I have been told by more than one prophetic person that I have been assigned an angelic escort who are powerful beings watching over me and protecting us as we have entered into spiritual warfare.

DISCORD TRANSFORMED AT THE GARDEN OF GETHSEMANE

At an earlier harp school we had a definitive experience in Jerusalem at the Dominus Flevit compound at the Garden of Gethsemane on the Mount of Olives. Let me describe the scene as our harp students arrived at this place where Jesus was in intercession and agony, sweating drops of blood just prior to His crucifixion. You would think that this would be a peaceful place where one could reflect and meditate on spiritual matters, but this was not the case. As we were setting up our harps and music stands, there was a cacophony of agitating sounds filling the air. Dogs were barking, tourists led by their guide were being given loud instructions with the use of a bullhorn, but worst of all the local mosque was spewing hateful words over their loudspeaker system. It was Friday morning, and normally mosques would be chanting prayers, but in this case the amplified shouting was inciting violence against the Jewish people.

We pulled out our harps and began to worship. Almost instantly, the atmosphere changed dramatically. The dogs stopped barking and the birds began to sing. As we initiated our worship and playing our harps in a specific key, the tourists began singing in the same key. We all began to look at each other and wonder what was going on. What was especially remarkable was that not only did the shouting from the mosque cease, the mu'addhin who had be ranting was now singing, also in the same key. Without a word of exaggeration this took place, and it was unquestionably noticeable to everyone who was there.

THE BALANCE TIPPED IN TUNISIA AS THE ARAB SPRING STARTS

As was mentioned, after giving instruction to the staff at the Jerusalem House of Prayer for All Nations (JHOPFAN) harps have become the primary musical instrument used during their prayer sets. It was during one of our times of harp intersession that an unusual anointing descended on our group. At JHOPFAN the nations are prayed for in rotation based on a system using the Gates of Jerusalem as a sort of clock that extends out to the four corners of the globe. It happened to be our turn to pray for the nations that extended through the Jaffa Gate, which includes North America and particularly the nation of Tunisia. Admittedly, none of us had prayed for that nation before, so we pulled out a book that detailed the current situation in that country and began to use our harps to pray with fervor into the needs of that nation with the beautiful sound of music on the harp. Only a short time after that, we found out that the Arab Spring broke out there in Tunisia, which has since had a domino effect that has radically changed the whole Muslim world.

Now, I don't presume that in that one moment of intercession we were singularly responsible for turning over this situation. However, as the bowls of prayer are filled in heaven with the intercessions of the saints around the world, who knows what final push in prayer could tip the balance of the destiny of nations as we intercede before the throne of God? This privilege is clearly indicated for us as believers in Psalm 149:

> *Praise the Lord! Sing to the Lord a new song, and His praise in the assembly of saints. Let Israel rejoice in their Maker; let the children of Zion be joyful in their King. Let them praise His name with the dance; let them sing praises to Him with the* **timbrel and harp.** *For the Lord takes pleasure in His people; He will beautify the humble with salvation. Let the saints be joyful in glory; let them sing aloud on their beds. Let the high praises of God be in their mouth, and a two-edged sword in their hand, to execute vengeance on the nations, and punishments on the peoples; to bind their kings with chains, and their nobles with fetters of iron; to execute on them the written judgment—this honor have all His saints. Praise the Lord!*

GOD'S SECRET END-TIME WEAPON

It may appear that harp music is a bit out of context for a book such as this; however, the concept of bringing a sound that vibrates with the chords of heaven is important as it relates to understanding this significant aspect of spiritual warfare. The harp has been conspicuously absent from use in the Church throughout the centuries. I believe that its restoration is one of God's secret end-time weapons and is part of the restoration of the Tabernacle of David promised in Amos 9. Again, this is the topic of another book.

This harping about harps may seem a bit narrow in perspective and application. Certainly similar results can be achieved using other instruments and other modes of prayer. What is noteworthy, however, is the manner in which the intention of worship is released through the vibrating strings and how that vibration echoes that which is found around the throne of God. The main thing we need to do is get on the same frequency of the supernatural that is happening in heaven and so be in sync with the power of God that He wants to release against the powers of darkness. Regardless, this harp paradigm is clearly indicated and uniquely expressed in the Bible.

Isaiah 30:32 corroborates this idea when it declares the use of harps as the judgements of the Lord are meted out:

> *And in every place where the staff of punishment passes, which the Lord lays on him, it will be with tambourines and harps.*

So why is the harp so particularly effective in the area of spiritual warfare and also deliverance? Let's look to the well-known story of David's harp playing and the relief that Saul experienced under the anointing that at least temporarily delivered the troubled king of Israel. We find this story in First Samuel:

> *Whenever the evil spirit from God bothered Saul, David would play his harp. Saul would relax and feel better, and the evil spirit would go away* (1 Samuel 16:23 CEV).

It may seem odd that this evil spirit is attributed to God; however, it is my understanding that Saul's lack of trust in God and his disobedience opened the door for this oppression (see 1 Sam. 15). Only in this sense does God allow the evil spirit to operate. In this manner we can see that the judgement and consequences that comes from Saul's rebellion are from God. This rebellion led to a spirit of fear, jealousy, and murder as he drifted further and further from God and ultimately to his demise. Despite the temporary relief Saul experienced when David played, the evil spirit always returned. This is indicative of what Jesus taught us in Matthew 12:43-45:

> When an unclean spirit goes out of a man, he goes through dry places, seeking rest, and finds none. Then he says, "I will return to my house from which I came." And when he comes, he finds it empty, swept, and put in order. Then he goes and takes with him seven other spirits more wicked than himself, and they enter and dwell there; and the last state of that man is worse than the first. So shall it also be with this wicked generation.

So what is it that the demons found so repulsive that they fled from the sound of the playing of David's harp? I believe that it was the sound of heaven. It must torment them to have to stay around and hear it. Certainly, it reminds them of their previous state prior to their fall and, of course, the fate that awaits them in the final judgement.

We know that as God inhabits our praise, God's presence pushes back the darkness. Surely, wherever God is present, evil cannot co-exist. That is why it is so important to surround ourselves with an atmosphere of praise and worship. Let's fill our homes, our cars, and our hearts with music that dispels the darkness. Worship music should not be confined to our church experience. We need to be diligent to not allow any media that will give demonic access to our lives through the music we listen to or what we expose ourselves to on the Internet, TV, or radio.

MASS DELIVERANCE IN TRINIDAD

As we conclude our discussion of deliverance, let me share a remarkable experience that relates to this topic that took place in Trinidad. This experience occurred during one of my first overseas ministry trips. This was at a time when I didn't have a harp that was easy to travel with. It therefore took special shipping arrangements with the president of the airline based in Trinidad. The large harp was placed in a crate that looked similar to a coffin, so the only stipulation given was that the crate had to be stood up on end so that it would not appear like we were shipping a cadaver. This is beside the point, but it was rather humorous.

I did manage to get around with the harp once I was on the ground, and for the most part the believers on the island had never seen a harp, let alone heard one played live. While in Trinidad I was a bit shocked—everywhere I went I saw many pagan shrines and temples where demon worship was practiced. The ministry was well received, and at one particular fellowship a most unusual thing happened during the altar call.

In a congregation of around 1,000 people, about 100 people came forward in a call for salvation and prayer. During this time, there was a beautiful sense of God's presence as I was ministering the lovely sound of worship on my harp. Suddenly, without warning, everyone standing at the front of the church fell flat down at the same instant, very much like dropping a handful of pick-up-sticks. It was as if a Holy Spirit bomb went off leveling everyone to the floor. From what I could see, most individuals were writhing like snakes on the ground. Being rather new to this at the time, I was amazed and wondered how bizarre this all seemed. Thankfully, the pastoral team took it all in stride and ministered freedom to these people, as it was common for people who were new to the faith to require deliverance from the demons they had previously worshiped.

Here in North America, the need for deliverance is no less. The manifestation of pagan altars may not be so obvious, but the altar of our screens is no less an entry point for the demonic. Family members spend countless hours in front of perverse games and images, making the necessity for the ministry of deliverance even more relevant for today.

Since then I have found the harp has played a wonderful role in my ministry to administer deliverance and physical healing. In a few incidents we have seen the lame walk and blind eyes see, and we long to see even more in the future as we release the lovely heavenly sound of the harp.

The closing scriptures I'd like to like share with you on this topic reveal a surprising fact—God Himself sings over us a song of deliverance. Zephaniah 3:17 tells us:

> *The Lord your God in your midst, the Mighty One, will save; He will rejoice over you with gladness, He will quiet you with His love, He will rejoice over you with singing.*

Wow, what a song that must be when the Creator of the universe sings a song of freedom over us. If it is God who spoke or maybe actually sung the worlds into existence, then what kind of creative force must be in play when He rejoices over us with singing? Truly, if the Son makes us free, then we are free indeed (see John 8:36)!

How is it, though, that we could hear His song on this side of heaven? Typically, it is up to those of us who have stewarded the prophetic tools given to us through the gifts of the Holy Spirit. As a prophetic harpist, it is my greatest joy to hear the music of heaven and translate it here on earth for all to hear. There is a wondrous release of heavenly music at this time in the history of the church and many technologies make it easier than ever to create and make it available through our computers. Let us all do what we can to fill the earth with frequencies of the supernatural that incorporate the songs of deliverance to set the captives free. Psalm 32:7 assures us:

You are my hiding place; You shall preserve me from trouble; You shall surround me with songs of deliverance. Selah.

CHAPTER SIXTEEN

PARADISE LOST,
PARADISE FOUND

It was the 60s and a generation went searching for their souls. Their anthem was heard at "Woodstock", the iconic three-day music festival that captured that zeitgeist. In the music of that era there was a sense of sincere longing, often even with spiritual overtones, that cried for freedom and a reversal of the tragic condition of the human soul as a result of the Fall in the Garden of Eden. This is a legitimate desire because God has placed eternity in our hearts:

> *He has made everything beautiful in its time. Also He has put eternity in their hearts, except that no one can find out the work that God does from beginning to end* (Ecclesiastes 3:11).

During this cultural revolution there was a desire to get "back to the earth," which is the very substance we were created from, and somehow regain the state of innocence that was lost when Adam and Eve sinned. Sadly, in truth, the path back to that state of innocence was shut with a flaming sword blocking the way back into Eden (see Gen. 3:24). The reality is that we cannot possibly get ourselves back to our original relationship with the Creator without His help.

There are a number of individuals who could be classed as "science popularizers"—such as Michio Kaku, Neil deGrasse Tyson, and the wacky but popular Bill Nye the Science Guy—who have had a significant influence in today's society. All too often, however, many such individuals have an anti-God bent and attempt to use science as a means to discredit belief in God. The truth is the scientific method of study can never prove or disprove the existence of God as God is beyond this dimension. It is a bit like the illustration of the cobbler who creates a shoe. Just because you cannot find the cobbler inside the shoe does not prove that the cobbler does not exist. This is despite the fact that the existence of the shoe suggests that there is a cobbler who made it. One such science popularizer was the late astrophysicist, author, and science communicator Carl Sagan whose public lectures likely inspired many of the songs of that era that referenced the cosmos. Here is a quote from Sagan's book entitled *The Cosmic Connection: An Extraterrestrial Perspective* published in 1973:

> Our Sun is a second- or third-generation star. All of the rocky and metallic material we stand on, the iron in our blood, the calcium in our teeth, the carbon in our genes were produced billions of years ago in the interior of a red giant star. We are made of star-stuff.[1]

So astrophysicists like Carl Sagan claim that supernovae are the source of the more complex chemical elements that are found in the universe and ultimately are part of the substance of the human body. This may actually be factual. God indeed allowed the stars to be formed, and in the eons of time He formed the heavier elements through the supernova of a star and used these elements during the formation of the earth. We read in Genesis how God did not simply materialize matter from nothing to create Adam's body but chose to form it from the dust of the earth. Genesis 2:7 details the construction of Adam's body and the energizing breath that imparted life to his soul:

And the Lord God formed man of the dust of the ground, and breathed into his nostrils the breath of life; and man became a living being.

Fresh from the hands of the Creator, Adam must have been an amazing creature. As mentioned before, his "bandwidth" to function on the frequency of the supernatural was free of any interference. His ability to resonate with his Creator was perfect, and communication as they walked in the cool of the evening was crystal clear. Adam's authority to have dominion on earth was unhindered by anything. He was perfect, and God said that it was good.

We notice in Genesis 2 that out of the ground the living creatures were also formed. But God had an ulterior motive as He gave Adam the task of naming the animals. Here we see Adam's fine intellect at work at a level beyond today's PhD zoologists. I wonder at what point after observing that each species had a male and female did he realize that God was showing him his own need for a mate?

And the Lord God said, "It is not good that man should be alone; I will make him a helper comparable to him." Out of the ground the Lord God formed every beast of the field and every bird of the air, and brought them to Adam to see what he would call them. And whatever Adam called each living creature, that was its name. So Adam gave names to all cattle, to the birds of the air, and to every beast of the field. But for Adam there was not found a helper comparable to him.

And the Lord God caused a deep sleep to fall on Adam, and he slept; and He took one of his ribs, and closed up the flesh in its place. Then the rib which the Lord God had taken from man He made into a woman, and He brought her to the man (Genesis 2:18-22).

I believe that the underlying meaning of this whole exercise was not just to make it obvious that God intended for Adam to see his need for a mate. The intent was to reveal that God was designing a means by which a bride for Himself could be obtained. The drama of human history and the passion of the Cross were to culminate ultimately in the calling out of the Bride of Christ. This magnificent cosmic conclusion is addressed in the final chapter of this book.

DE-EVOLUTION AND THE FALL OF MAN

Those who hold to the theory of evolution say that we evolved from lower forms of life becoming more complex over time, but in a sense the opposite is true. Prior to the Fall, man was at his highest level of connection with his Creator. His ability to be a resident of this dimension as a soul in a perfect body and to simultaneously be fully alive to the heavenly dimension was truly awesome. One can only imagine what Adam was capable of as the words and intent of his unblemished soul and spirit could be expressed in a pure form that must have functioned spectacularly on a quantum level. There was no cancer that could harm his body as his DNA was perfect. The sun's harmful rays were perfectly shielded by the mist that hung about the whole earth (see Gen. 2:6). It was paradise.

The great tragedy that occurred at the Fall started a downward spiral for mankind on a quantum level. Paradise had been lost. A spiritual de-evolution commenced and, as the generations went by, on a physical level even the lifespan of mankind slowly decreased. Once out of sync with his Creator, this once fully connected spirit-being living in a perfect body now experienced a painful separation from the loving Light that formed him.

The great Christian theologian Watchman Nee, in his master-piece treatise *The Spiritual Man*, comments on this in the third chapter under the heading "Soul and Body after the Fall." Here, Nee describes how man in his original state of innocence was first led by his spirit, which subjugated the soul and consequently the body. After the Fall, the order of the chain of command in man's being was reversed and the body's cravings dominated the soul, and the spirit of man was no longer alive to God. Here is a direct quote from this classic book:

> Adam lived by the breath of life becoming spirit in him. By the spirit he sensed God, knew God's voice, and communed with God. He had a very keen awareness of God. But after his fall his spirit died.
>
> When God spoke to Adam at the first He said, "in the day that you eat of it (the fruit of the tree of good and evil) you shall die" (Gen. 2.17). Adam and Eve neverthe-less continued on for hundreds of years after eating the

forbidden fruit. This obviously indicates that the death God foretold was not physical. Adam's death began in his spirit.[2]

The good news is there is redemption, and the connection Adam originally had with God can be restored. This, in fact, was God's plan from the start. Again, as God is the Master of time and space, as the Alpha and the Omega He knew the beginning from the end, or rather we should say He knew the end from the beginning. Adam's fall was no surprise to God. The high price that is paid to gift mankind with a free will innately carries with it the potential to choose to not obey God's will. This supreme gift is what it takes to have the capacity to love because without the ability to choose good or evil, it is not possible to have the ability to love.

What did it take to restore Adam? What covered their nakedness? It was through the shed blood of an animal, which is a picture of the redemption that was to come:

Also for Adam and his wife the Lord God made tunics of skin, and clothed them (Genesis 3:21).

What is indicated here is that through the sacrificing of an animal's life and the shedding of its blood a covering was made by God Himself that would clothe them. Hence, the principle of a substitutionary atonement is established. This is a picture of the ultimate redemption that would come through the shedding of blood by Jesus the Messiah, the Lamb who was slain before the foundations of the earth. These tunics of skin, just as Abraham was provided a ram instead of his son, were a prophetic foreshadowing of the redemption that was to come.

So we can summarize that at the Fall, Adam lost his capacity to resonate in union with God and his bandwidth was disrupted. Sin was the interference that limited his ability to be in sync with his Creator. The great good news of the Gospel is that the work that was accomplished at the Cross restored our ability to be in union with God. The issue of sin and its consequential effect of separating us from God is dealt with. The concept of intent that has been the major theme of our discussion of God's quantum universe is addressed in a powerful way through the Cross. What was God's intent in the drama that was set on the stage of the cosmos? God's intent was to create a dimension in time and space where we could come into existence and experience His love. In the light of what was done on the Cross, we can see that deep question of knowing the way that we can approach God, who was previously unapproachable, is answered. John 14:1-6 shows us that Jesus is the way:

> *"Let not your heart be troubled; you believe in God, believe also in Me. In My Father's house are many mansions; if it were not so, I would have told you. I go to prepare a place for you. And if I go and prepare a place for you, I will come again and receive you to Myself; that where I am, there you may be also. And where I go you know, and the way you know." Thomas said to Him, "Lord, we do not know where You are going, and how can we know the way?" Jesus said to him, "I am the way, the truth, and the life. No one comes to the Father except through Me."*

So we see that Jesus is the way to restoring the paradise that was lost and that He is the actual mechanism by which paradise is found. Surrendering your heart to the Lord is the gateway to getting in touch with the frequency of the supernatural. However, even after this initial handing over of your life to your Creator, there are many things that can hinder your bandwidth from fully operating. The following chapter will discuss some of these hindrances and will show how your spiritual bandwidth can be increased. This widening of your capacity to receive more from God will be the portal to the miraculous.

NOTES

1. Carl Sagan, *The Cosmic Connection: An Extraterrestrial Perspective* (Cambridge: Cambridge University Press, 2000), 190.

2. Watchman Nee, *The Spiritual Man* (New York: Christian Fellowship Publishers, 1968), 50.

CHAPTER SEVENTEEN

SPIRITUAL COGNITIVE DISSONANCE

In psychology, *cognitive dissonance* is a term used to describe a state of mental stress or discomfort that people experience if their beliefs, ideas, or values contradict each other. It also applies to someone who performs an action that is contrary to their beliefs, or a person can experience dissonance when they are confronted by new information that conflicts with their current beliefs, ideas, or values.

Dissonance is an appropriate term for the emotional lack of harmony in the soul since the Fall. In music, dissonance describes notes that are not in harmony with each other. From the perspective of an analysis of the frequencies of notes that are in harmony, the waveforms are mathematically in a perfect ratio to each other. For instance, two notes that sound as a major third interval in relation to each other are five to four. If you viewed two such tones on an oscilloscope (the device most often associated with the viewing of waveforms) you would observe that the peaks of the waveforms would fit evenly within each other at that ratio (see Illustration #14). These illustrations show examples of waveforms within waveforms—octave (2:1), perfect fifth (3:2), perfect fourth (4:3), major third (5:4), minor third (6:5), and whole tone (9:8).

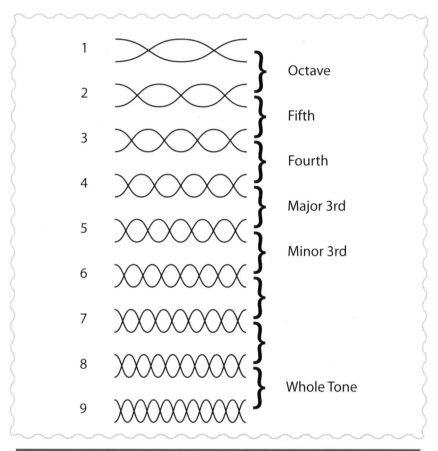

ILLUSTRATION #14: HARMONIC WAVEFORMS

The number on the left indicates the fundamental frequency or cycle over time. I have placed one wave over the other so that it is easier to envision. You can imagine a string drawn tight and plucked as it vibrates up and then down. "1" is one cycle, "2" is twice as fast sounding an octave higher and each ensuing interval is shown on the right. You can see how they fit perfectly in relationship to each other. The actual effect that is heard when two waveforms at the shown ratio are sounded together is obviously in harmony with each other. It is interesting to note that a string at a given length and tension will vibrate with these overtones in these ratios.

God made it so that when we hear these frequencies resonating together in specific ratios, we recognize them as pleasant and harmonious. Certain other intervals that are not at these ratios can sound discordant.

In the world of music, even if you are not a musician, your ear would recognize the harmonious sound of the intervals between two sounding notes at these ratios. Though it is hard to envision through just words and images, it is clear that these ratios are mathematically perfectly related to each other.

So it is with our souls. As the thoughts in our minds, emotions, and souls are not in agreement with God and what we understand in His Word, it could be said that we are not in resonance with Him. We are not on the same spiritual frequency. We are out of sync with Him, and we have the dissonance of the frequency of unbelief or, at the very least, a cacophony of spiritual frequencies.

The frequency of the supernatural is experienced when we resonate with a true understanding of God through His Word and an intimate relationship with Him through Jesus, the Messiah. Anyone who experiences what I call *spiritual cognitive dissonance* will have a discordance between what we believe in our intellect and what is really in our hearts. Our head knowledge is not in union with what our hearts truly experience. Sadly, this dissonance is something that we actually may not even be aware of. The greater the disconnect between these two realities, the more dysfunctional a person we are. This is true of issues that are on a soul level and can be addressed on a psychological level. However, when we relate to God and our understanding of spiritual principles, this can greatly affect our spiritual relationship with God and ultimately lead to a toxic spiritual and emotional condition.

There are many factors in our souls that determine our ability to be on the same spiritual frequency as God. When we read and hear God's Word, we can easily be in intellectual agreement with the words and concepts we hear, but in our heart of hearts we are unable to embrace the realities that God wants us to experience. For example, if we were raised in a family where the father was distant or abusive, when we become a believer it may be difficult to experience the love of God as our heavenly Father. In fact, such a person may be unable to address God as Father without projecting onto Him aspects of the dysfunctional relationship of their earthly father. This is spiritual cognitive dissonance. Intellectually, this person may think God is love, but when it comes to relating to Him in prayer, there is this nagging sensation that God will respond grudgingly to any requests. Perhaps there is a sense of performance orientation that cannot be overcome.

We can be set free from this kind of spiritual disconnect by getting in union with God. By synchronizing our mind, emotions, and spirit with Him we can achieve harmony in our beings. This can be achieved by the renewing of our mind through God's Word (see Rom. 12:2) and therefore getting our thoughts into agreement with His Word. However, as we seek Him in prayer we will likely require the help of mature believers who are familiar with the gifts of the Holy Spirit. As we are more often than not unaware of the spiritual dissonance we are in bondage to, we need to have prayer counseling. During times of personal prayer ministry, experienced prayer counselors will operate in the gift of words of knowledge and the discerning of spirits (see 1 Cor. 12:7-10), helping to reveal the lies that we believe that are putting us out of sync with God.

At the back of this book, I have an appendix that recommends a number of ministries and books that relate to the subject of inner healing. This area of understanding has helped countless individuals to be set free from their spiritual and emotional cognitive dissonance.

One of the most important aspects of this spiritual realignment is what we believe about ourselves in contrast to how God sees us from His perspective. If we see ourselves as victims rather than victors, we are unable to rise above the low bandwidth of lack of self-esteem. The solution to this is far more complex than simply changing the self-talk of our minds. Many self-improvement lecturers, motivational speakers, and self-help practitioners offer many practical ways to try to address dysfunctional mindsets; however, they are unable to fully address the damage caused by sin that is often generational in nature. This is the primary difference between positive thinking, often associated with New Age teaching, and what we as followers of Jesus ascribe to. Jesus is the way and the means by which we are healed and our souls are brought back into proper alignment with Him, ourselves, and others. He alone knows the key that will unlock our hearts, and only through Him can we be reconciled to God. He addresses not just the soul but goes to the very root of our spirits and, like Adam who was a lifeless lump of dirt, breathes life into us.

A message that I have shared all over the world in my travels is entitled "The Stone of Destiny" and it is based on Revelation 2:17:

> *He who has an ear, let him hear what the Spirit says to the churches. To him who overcomes I will give some of the hidden manna to eat. And I will give him a white stone, and on the stone a new name written which no one knows except him who receives it.*

This scripture speaks of our individual identity and destiny, which will be revealed in an amazing moment when Jesus presents to us this mystical white stone. No doubt this stone will bear a name that will encompass the way He sees us, and that name will perfectly describe who we are in Him in a most intimate way. On this side of heaven, however, the level of spiritual and emotional cognitive dissonance could be measured by the difference between the name with which the Lord defines us and the way we actually perceive ourselves. Here is a classic example of this found right in the pages of Scripture.

Judges 6:11 tells us the story of Gideon who is hiding in a winepress threshing some wheat, just eking out a means of staying alive and hiding in fear of the Midianites. The Lord makes an appearance and makes this outlandish declaration:

> And the Angel of the Lord appeared to him, and said to him, "The Lord is with you, you mighty man of valor!" (Judges 6:12)

Gideon is shocked and amazed by this statement and begins a dialogue with the Creator of the universe:

> Gideon said to Him, "O my lord, if the Lord is with us, why then has all this happened to us? And where are all His miracles which our fathers told us about, saying, 'Did not the Lord bring us up from Egypt?' But now the Lord has forsaken us and delivered us into the hands of the Midianites."
>
> Then the Lord turned to him and said, "Go in this might of yours, and you shall save Israel from the hand of the Midianites. Have I not sent you?"
>
> So he said to Him, "O my Lord, how can I save Israel? Indeed my clan is the weakest in Manasseh, and I am the least in my father's house."

And the Lord said to him, "Surely I will be with you, and you shall defeat the Midianites as one man" (Judges 6:13-16).

There is a sharp contrast between what God says about Gideon and the way Gideon perceives himself based on the very real circumstances of his life. God, however, speaks prophetic words of destiny, which ultimately become a reality. Even though there is a huge contradiction in God's perspective compared to Gideon's current state, God speaks into his destiny and a transformation takes place. We also can experience this transformation when we seek out the one who would speak words of life into us. His promise is found in Jeremiah 29:11-13:

For I know the thoughts that I think toward you, says the Lord, thoughts of peace and not of evil, to give you a future and a hope. Then you will call upon Me and go and pray to Me, and I will listen to you. And you will seek Me and find Me, when you search for Me with all your heart.

When we embrace the reality of the benevolent intent that God has for us, we can have confidence that we will encounter Him. Our part is to bring to bear our intent to search for Him with all our heart, and He promises that we will find Him. What is the implication of finding the Lord? This implication is that He will give us a hope and a future that only a God who is beyond time and space can guarantee. What a wonderful promise that encompasses divine intervention in your life and a release of the supernatural.

Once one's spiritual and emotional cognitive dissonance is addressed, our spiritual bandwidth is widened and we are in a position to function more freely in the frequency of the supernatural.

This transformation of our souls resets the order of the chain of command in our being as alluded to in the previous chapter. When God has touched us at the deepest level of our being, then we are properly aligned with Him and the pre-eminence of our spirits overtakes the previous dominance of body and soul. This process that we go through takes time and intentional effort as we work out our relationship with God. One thing is for sure, it is worth the effort!

CHAPTER EIGHTEEN

THE QUANTUM COUNTERFEIT

At this moment, it is worth considering the meaning of the word *counterfeit*. The *Merriam-Webster Dictionary* defines the word *counterfeit* as "made in imitation of something else with intent to deceive: forged, counterfeit money, a counterfeit diamond."[1] An article on this subject on Wikipedia makes this insightful statement: "Counterfeit products are often produced with the intent to take advantage of the superior value of the imitated product."[2]

When there is something that has authentic value, there is the risk that someone will take advantage of you and try to sell you something that appears to be the real thing but, in fact, is a fake. This is true not only of manufactured goods and even currency but also of truth. Various cults and religions will lay claim to the name and person of Jesus and incorporate their spin of who they claim Him to be in an attempt to use His credibility to endorse the heresy they promote. They are preaching "another Jesus" and a counterfeit Gospel as it states in Second Corinthians 11:3-4:

> *But I fear, lest somehow, as the serpent deceived Eve by his craftiness, so your minds may be corrupted from the simplicity that is in Christ. For if he who comes preaches another Jesus whom we have not preached, or if you receive a different spirit which you have not received, or a different gospel which you have not accepted—you may well put up with it!*

There is an old Latin phrase that is well known even to this day that says *caveat emptor*: "Let the buyer beware." Throughout human history there has been a need to be careful about what we buy into. Apparently, as we see from our reading of the above scripture, right from the Garden there has been the need to closely examine the goods we are being sold. What is particularly deceptive is that the counterfeit has been craftily designed to appear authentic. We need to keep in mind that where there is a counterfeit, there is something of real value that has been copied. After all, we don't throw away money just because there are counterfeit bills floating around. The important thing is that we must develop our understanding of the Bible so that we will be able to discern what is valid.

As a starting point in our discussion of the *quantum counterfeit*, I'd like to share with you an observation that I made while researching the zero-point energy topic. I encountered an article that, from a scientific point of view, was one of the best summations of this topic. Unfortunately, by the end of this article, the subject wandered into New Age thought. To be precise, the author made a statement that equated thought with energy and energy with matter and concluded that by thinking you can create matter. I'm choosing to not mention the author's name as I do not want to seem to put down this individual personally. This individual's credentials were impressive as far as education and philanthropy. His bio even mentioned him having a Christian upbringing. As a highly sought out motivational speaker he has appeared alongside some of the most well-known names. However, after doing a quick search of his books on Amazon, I found that his material was classified as "New Age & Spirituality > New Thought > Religion & Spirituality > Occult." The true colors of this author are made plain through the many publications in which he references his experiences with Buddhist monks and his articulate musings on quantum physics. By appearing knowledgeable about quantum physics, his New Age message gains credibility by association. This is why it is important, as we sift through the vast amount of information on the subject of quantum physics, that we use discernment and not just accept at face value every thought that is presented.

Truthfully, Christianity certainly has elements of the metaphysical that we should not hesitate to embrace. We have made it clear that the supernatural should be a natural part of the believer's life experience as we walk and talk with God. The difference between New Age philosophy and what the Bible teaches is that we believe in God who is a person and not an inanimate force in the universe. We do not base our faith on a universe that is responding to "good or bad vibrations" that we give out as people, even though our relationship with the Lord of the universe gives us a very positive outlook on life. We believe in a Creator who made the universe, not some universal consciousness. When we base our faith on God and His Word, we are not just calling on some positive energy; we are aligning our hearts with a being who loves us, communicates with us, and relates to us on an intimate level.

There is a plethora of material on the Internet that utilizes quantum jargon that seeks to claim scientific credibility for their particular philosophy. At the risk of seeming to fall into the same category, I have attempted in this book to make clear what is science, what is supernatural, and where they intersect. I make no apology for the mystical aspects of Christianity, for we truly have a supernatural God, and the claims of the Bible are radical but not beyond reason. What is critical in our discussion is the ideology that has been defined as quantum mysticism, which is based on pseudo-scientific concepts. Quantum mysticism essentially seeks to relate quantum mechanics to consciousness, intelligence, spirituality, or mystical worldviews. Generally, it is rejected by scientists. Let me give you a few examples of how this philosophy has become pervasive in today's popular culture.

It seems that every self-help author and speaker has a book to sell with their brand of "quantum something." The 2006 bestseller *The Secret* edited by Rhonda Byrne is no exception. This book sold over 20 million copies partially due to her appearance on *The Oprah Winfrey Show*. However, numerous authors with credentials that include Harvard and *The New York Times* have rejected Byrne's comments on quantum physics as having no scientific basis.

In an article entitled *"The Secret* Exposed" by Mel Lawrenz we read:

> You can gain anything you want in life—wealth, health, the perfect mate, business success, respect from others—literally anything. That is the promise of the No. 1 best-selling book *The Secret (Beyond Words)*. The editor, Rhonda Byrne, explains that "the secret" can be found in everything from Babylonian religion to Buddhism to Albert Einstein. *The Secret* (available as both a book and a DVD) is no secret now, however. It has become a

global video event, a clever cross-promotional marketing plan, and a book touted by Oprah.[3]

The Secret, in a nutshell, is what has come to be known as "the law of attraction," which basically states that whatever you think you will attract to yourself in reality. Sadly, many Christians do not discern the spirit behind this philosophy. This has grown out of publications such as the grandfather of positive thinking self-help books *Psycho-Cybernetics* by Maxwell Maltz written in 1960. Many personal development experts such as Zig Ziglar, Tony Robbins, and Brian Tracy have based their teaching on this foundational book.

One of the most well-known purveyors of this New Age thought is Deepak Chopra. This is particularly true in his book *Quantum Healing* where he tries to use quantum theory to explain that aging is caused by the mind. In an exposé on YouTube, Richard Dawkins suggests that Chopra is "exploiting quantum jargon as plausible sounding hocus-pocus."[4]

The common thread in these pervasive lines of New Age thought is the idea of the self changing the self. Watchman Nee used the term *soulish* to describe this dangerous fallen human condition:

> A very common expression of a soulish walk manifests itself in the will—that power of self-assertion. Through it believers who live in the soul make self the center of every thought, word and action. They want to know for *their* satisfaction, feel for *their* enjoyment, labor according to *their* plan. The hub of their life is self and the ultimate aim is to glorify themselves.[5]

It is a vain approach to attempt to affect a change in the soul through human effort. Often, at the heart of this false teaching there is a caveat that if one only realized that they are divine then this revelation would place them on a higher plane and they would rise above their problems and become enlightened. In other words, you are God. What is rather ironic about this term *New Age* is that there is actually nothing new about it. It all originated in the Garden of Eden and the age-old temptation that satan first tempted Eve with.

Genesis 3 recounts for us that tragic day and the sly approach satan took to snare Eve. What could he best tempt Eve with? It was nothing less that the promise of godhood.

> *Now the serpent was more cunning than any beast of the field which the Lord God had made. And he said to the woman, "Has God indeed said, 'You shall not eat of every tree of the garden'?"*
>
> *And the woman said to the serpent, "We may eat the fruit of the trees of the garden; but of the fruit of the tree which is in the midst of the garden, God has said, 'You shall not eat it, nor shall you touch it, lest you die.'"*
>
> *Then the serpent said to the woman, "You will not surely die. For God knows that in the day you eat of it your eyes will be opened, and you will be like God, knowing good and evil"* (Genesis 3:1-5).

Here satan attempts to sell Eve a counterfeit. Why wouldn't Eve want to be "like God"? Satan knew that this would appeal to her the most, and of course we know the rest of the story. So it appears that satan has not changed his deceptive story and still offers the old line, only packaged in the so-called New Age with promises of divinity. Sadly, people are still falling for this line and end up shutting out the God who longs to restore them to a true experience of His love and the bona fide frequency of the supernatural.

In truth we still must not eat of the tree of the knowledge of good and evil as its root is corrupt and leads to self-effort and death. That is why discernment is so needful, especially when wading through the minefield of quantum counterfeits. This corrupted tree can only fill us with esoteric knowledge and only connect us with half-truths that reach only our mind and soul. God wants so much more for us. He wants us to have an authentic relationship with Him that promises us that we can become a member of His family as a son or daughter. He wants our spirit to come alive through the regeneration that comes through the Cross. By partaking of the tree of the knowledge of good and evil we try to circumvent the Cross. However, by embracing the Cross we encounter the way that legitimately leads to the Tree of Life—and everlasting life. Desiring godhood as presented in New Age thought flatters the soul and is a counterfeit. The real value offered in the Gospel is that by humbling yourself and accepting the way of salvation that God devised from the beginning of time, the way is opened back to the Garden.

FREQUENCY NON-SCIENCE

In conclusion of our discussion on the topic of quantum counterfeits, I have a few parting thoughts. People are constantly asking me about certain specific uses of musical vibrations with a spiritual undertone that are, frankly, non-science or actually nonsense. Certainly, these spurious practices should be exposed in a book entitled *The Frequency of the Supernatural*. In the example that I am about to address, there is an underlying premise that falls apart when thought through logically. Consequently, we should not buy into the CDs and related material purported to have some mystical quality inherent to the products.

One such example of this is promoted on a website hosted by a musician who claims that music composed and produced around specific frequencies has an innate healing power. He claims that God gave him this music and even makes reference to special information that was given to him in Israel by a Jewish person—as if somehow, by association, this makes this information a credible supernatural source. He also claims that these frequencies are the same tones that King David himself used when, in fact, there is no possible way of knowing the exact frequencies that an ancient instrument was tuned to. It is personally troublesome to me as a harp instructor who teaches the psalms of David that the mystery of King David is exploited to sell this man's CDs.

What is sad is that even though we cannot know the exact tuning standard that David used, the Bible does have musical markings written into the actual Hebrew text that indicate the ancient melody that can be played to reveal the original melody that was penned. This discovery was made by a Jewish musicologist, the late Suzanne Haïk-Vantoura, whose life work was to examine the "cantillation pointings" found in the Old Testament. Her scholarly work *Music of the Bible Revealed* explains in detail how theses tones were decoded and how existing ancient synagogue music matches her findings. In my harp schools, I teach my harp students how to play these ancient melodies using these markings that carry a powerful anointing through the original music. I discuss this in detail in my book *As It Is in Heaven*. The inaccurate use of King David's so-called frequencies contrasted to the magnificent credible discovery of the "cantillation pointings" is an example of how a counterfeit can risk actually discrediting something that is valid.

Again, I am intentionally leaving out the name of this individual. I find it distasteful to even have to bring up the subject; however, this must be addressed. On his website are numerous testimonials of the healing power found in his musical recordings on a series of CDs. Each CD is centered around the instruments playing music that is tuned to a certain tuning standard and key signature, and he claims that this tuning heals specific ailments. He offers a series of DVDs featuring color-coordinated imagery, also purporting to somehow match the music frequencies and consequently have a therapeutic value. Promising healing based on certain tones is sadly misleading and self-serving despite the spiritual language. I cannot endorse this premise, especially as he is making money off desperate people looking for healing from anywhere they may find it. The only true healer is Jesus, and He does not need any special frequencies to do it.

This idea that a special pseudoscientific effect is gained by retuning our instruments to different tuning standards has been circulating on the Internet for some time. The concept, for example, is rather than tuning to the standard A = 440 hertz that was agreed upon in 1955 by the International Organization for Standardization, that mystical qualities can be attained by tuning A = 432 hertz. A conspiracy theory has also been attributed to this shifting of tuning standards that has to do with Nazis somehow having a hand in making this change to purposely make the world more anxious. Sadly, this is all nonsense. Such a small change in frequency is hardly noticeable let alone somehow changing the spiritual dynamic of music played using this tuning standard.

A COUNTERFEIT IMITATES SOMETHING REAL

As was stated at the beginning of this chapter, where there is a counterfeit, there is something real that has value. When a Spirit-filled musician is ministering in music under the anointing of God, God's healing power is released. I have seen blind eyes see and the lame jump for joy under the influence of such godly music. The beautiful frequencies that have a heavenly origin can be played in a live setting and even captured on a digital recording and the power of God can flow even when the recording is played back at a later time. Let's buy that CD! Specific tones, rhythms, and melodies that are Spirit-breathed during worship can lift a gathering of believers truly into the heavenly realms. I exhort all ministers of music to seek to enter into the courts of heaven and bring to earth a taste of the music in heaven.

The use of color during these times of worship—incorporating banners, billows of fabric, streamers, and lighting—can enhance a release of God's presence. My invention of the electronic harp, called the Harpella, is made from clear acrylic and lights up with the colors of the rainbow when it is played. It can be deliberately set to radiate specifically in synchronization with the music with the intent of tapping into the colors that have prophetic meaning. In times of intense spiritual warfare, the color red, indicative of the blood of Jesus, can be accessed. Gold colors speak of the glory of God. Purple represents royalty. Blues speak of heaven. The whole range of the frequency of colors can express a myriad of moods and meanings that all point to the Creator of the universe who intended that we make use of music and color in a creative and intelligent way to express the wondrous facets of the Kingdom of God. Let us not settle for some cheap imitation of the reality of the frequency of the supernatural!

NOTES

1. Merriam-Webster.com, s.v. "Counterfeit," accessed January 31, 2018, https://www.merriam-webster.com/dictionary/counterfeit.

2. "Counterfeit," Wikipedia, January 27, 2018, https://en.wikipedia.org/wiki/Counterfeit.

3. Mel Lawrenz, "The Secret Exposed," ChristianityToday.com, June 18, 2007, http://www.christianitytoday.com/ct/2007/june/20.71.html.

4. 77GSlinger, "Quantum Quacks: Part 1, Richard Dawkins Exposes Quantum Charlatan Deepak Chopra," YouTube, December 18, 2010, https://www.youtube.com/watch?v=jfVIl1UUQns.

5. Nee, *The Spiritual Man,* 168.

CHAPTER NINETEEN

THE END OF ALL THINGS

As it was appropriate for us to start our discussion of quantum physics "in the beginning" by referencing the Genesis account of creation, so, as we come to a close, we should consider the end of all things and the ultimate destiny of the universe and our place in it. Genesis 1:1-2 tells us:

> *In the beginning God created the heavens and the earth. The earth was without form, and void; and darkness was on the face of the deep. And the Spirit of God was hovering over the face of the waters.*

From an astrophysicist's point of view, this describes a time when the earth did not exist and the "deep" was dark and void. So in the beginning, before the creation, there was nothing. But what will happen in the end? Astronomers have a number of theories of how it will all end, but the Bible offers some hints:

> *All the host of heaven shall be dissolved, and the heavens shall be rolled up like a scroll; all their host shall fall down as the leaf falls from the vine, and as fruit falling from a fig tree* (Isaiah 34:4).

And in Revelation 6:13-14 we are given a similar grim prognosis:

> *And the stars of heaven fell to the earth, as a fig tree drops its late figs when it is shaken by a mighty wind. Then the sky receded as a scroll when it is rolled up, and every mountain and island was moved out of its place.*

Even Jesus Himself uses language that, from a cosmological perspective, speaks of apocalyptic events that are shortly to come to pass. Matthew 24:29 tells us:

> *Immediately after the tribulation of those days the sun will be darkened, and the moon will not give its light; the stars will fall from heaven, and the powers of the heavens will be shaken.*

Regardless of one's interpretation of the events described in these scriptures, either literal or poetic in language or a bit of both, here we see that something cataclysmic will take place at the end of all things.

There are many astrophysicists who offer little hope for the future of our universe as they theorize how things will come to an end. Most say that it is fortunate that this will be billions or even trillions of years in the future so we won't be around to see it come to pass.

What then is the cosmic forecast for the future of the universe? One such forecast is widely scattered periods of dark, followed by a complete dispersion of nothingness. This scenario has been called the "Big Freeze." This theory seems to be held by the majority of astrophysics. Based on the observation of a universe that continues to expand, the ultimate end of it all would indicate the breakdown of all matter scattered over an infinite universe where temperatures approach absolute zero. As the matter that normally forms stars is exhausted, the universe will get darker and darker. All matter will fall into black holes, but even these will eventually "evaporate" as they emit what is called *Hawking radiation*. A final state of high entropy will leave the universe a vast void. It appears that things will end up like they started according to this theory of the end of all things.

Another variation of the theme is called "The Big Rip." Here it is hypothesized that at a time in the distant future all matter and even space-time itself is ripped apart due to the expansion of the universe. The end result is a great emptiness of space.

Yet another theory that again seems to "bookend" all of time is called the "Big Crunch." In the Big Crunch the determining factor that would indicate if this scenario will occur is the density of the universe. If the universe ultimately is dense enough, the expansion will eventually reverse due to gravitational forces and "crunch" back on itself. If this is the case, then some have postulated that the cosmos is an "oscillatory universe" where Big Bangs and Big Crunches cycle infinitely. It has also been suggested that this cycle is not infinite and that due to the second law of thermodynamics entropy would increase with each oscillation and ultimately end in a big freeze, also called *heat death*.

So it appears that "our density is our destiny" or in reverse you could say our universe's destiny is in its density. (This reminds me of a funny moment in the movie *Back to the Future*. The lead character,

Marty, has a geeky father who absent-mindedly says something similar to Marty's future mother: "You are my *density*" instead of "destiny.") Interestingly enough, astrophysicists use the Greek letter Omega (Ω) to designate the parameter of the density of the universe. Of course, Jesus referred to Himself in Revelation 1:8, 21:6, and 22:13 as the "Alpha and Omega." So it is fitting that the outcome of the entire history of the universe is determined by this factor.

If the universe is "flat," it means that the average density is equal to a critical value and if these two values are divided together the Ω value is 1. A flat universe will expand indefinitely. If the critical value is less than the average density then the Ω value is less than 1, in which case the universe is called "open" and will also continue to expand forever. So if the Ω value is 1 or less, one of our first two scenarios will occur—either Big Freeze or Big Rip. However, if the critical value is larger than the average density, the Ω is 1+. That being the case, we are destined for a Big Crunch. In this case, the universe is considered to be "closed."

Despite the doom and gloom given to us from these theories of the end, there is a great hope that is described in the Bible:

> *Now I saw a new heaven and a new earth, for the first heaven and the first earth had passed away. Also there was no more sea. Then I, John, saw the holy city, New Jerusalem, coming down out of heaven from God, prepared as a bride adorned for her husband. And I heard a loud voice from heaven saying, "Behold, the tabernacle of God is with men, and He will dwell with them, and they shall be His people. God Himself will be with them and be their God. And God will wipe away every tear from their eyes; there shall be no more death, nor sorrow, nor crying. There shall be no more pain, for the former things have passed away."*

Then He who sat on the throne said, "Behold, I make all things new." And He said to me, "Write, for these words are true and faithful."

And He said to me, "It is done! I am the Alpha and the Omega, the Beginning and the End. I will give of the fountain of the water of life freely to him who thirsts. He who overcomes shall inherit all things, and I will be his God and he shall be My son" (Revelation 21:1-7).

At the edge of time there is a new age dawning, but it is not the "New Age" that those who hold this occult philosophy are expecting. It is the final intersection of the dimension of heaven and our earthly dimension. The age-old prayer that says, "As it is in heaven, let it be here on earth," will actually come into reality when these dimensional planes intersect in the New Jerusalem.

Revelation 21:9-11 describes our first contact with heaven in what appears to be what one could imagine as a massive inter-dimensional spacecraft:

"Come, I will show you the bride, the Lamb's wife." And he carried me away in the Spirit to a great and high moun-tain, and showed me the great city, the holy Jerusalem, descending out of heaven from God, having the glory of God.

Verse 16 of this same chapter defines the enormous size in today's measurements as being 1,380 miles by 1,380 miles. This is about the distance from the US-Canada border to the US-Mexico border and could either be in the shape of a cube (*Star Trek* fans may have a Borg cube come to mind) or pyramid according to the following description:

The city is laid out as a square; its length is as great as its breadth. And he measured the city with the reed: twelve thousand furlongs. Its length, breadth, and height are equal (Revelation 21:16).

What is most amazing is, in direct contrast to the dismal predictions of the fate of the universe as suggested in the Big Freeze, all will not end in darkness. In fact, the apostle John makes a most remarkable observation of a cosmic celestial phenomenon in Revelation 21:22-26:

But I saw no temple in it, for the Lord God Almighty and the Lamb are its temple. The city had no need of the sun or of the moon to shine in it, for the glory of God illuminated it. The Lamb is its light. And the nations of those who are saved shall walk in its light, and the kings of the earth bring their glory and honor into it. Its gates shall not be shut at all by day (there shall be no night there). And they shall bring the glory and the honor of the nations into it.

The final state of the universe will not lack for light as the Lord of light who originated all energy and matter will by His very person be the source of light. In the very final moments of the universe as we know it, the apostle Peter makes this astronomical pronouncement:

But the day of the Lord will come as a thief in the night, in which the heavens will pass away with a great noise, and the elements will melt with fervent heat; both the earth and the works that are in it will be burned up (2 Peter 3:10).

The promise is that for all of eternity we have the security of knowing that the Creator of the universe intended from the beginning of time to design a place for all those who love Him. And so we see that the end is but the beginning.

At the end of the Bible, Jesus offers this invitation and warning in Revelation 22:12-17:

> *"And behold, I am coming quickly, and My reward is with Me, to give to every one according to his work. I am the Alpha and the Omega, the Beginning and the End, the First and the Last." Blessed are those who do His commandments, that they may have the right to the tree of life, and may enter through the gates into the city. But outside are dogs and sorcerers and sexually immoral and murderers and idolaters, and whoever loves and practices a lie. "I, Jesus, have sent My angel to testify to you these things in the churches. I am the Root and the Offspring of David, the Bright and Morning Star." And the Spirit and the bride say, "Come!" And let him who hears say, "Come!" And let him who thirsts come. Whoever desires, let him take the water of life freely.*

We are all offered the invitation to be a part of God's family as a son or daughter. However, the offer is conditional upon accepting it and receiving it freely without earning it. Jesus gives us a wonderful promise of the consummation of time:

> *And He said to me, "It is done! I am the Alpha and the Omega, the Beginning and the End. I will give of the fountain of the water of life freely to him who thirsts. He*

who overcomes shall inherit all things, and I will be his God and he shall be My son" (Revelation 21:6-7).

THE KARDASHEV SCALE AND THE CULTURE OF THE KING OF THE UNIVERSE

As a parting thought I wanted to contrast a final scientific concept with the King of the universe who is the true Master of the frequency of the supernatural and the natural realms. The Kardashev scale is a theoretical measure of a civilization's capability to harness the energy available to them through their technology. Many science fiction fans have a hope that one day mankind would develop to the highest levels of the type of culture envisioned by this scale. Here are the levels and a point form list of what a civilization should have achieved to attain a given type of culture. Sadly, we have not even attained the first level. Perhaps, as we come into the fullness of the eternal plans of God, we are destined to rise to the level where we can explore God's infinite universe unhindered by the limitations of our current technologies.

CIVILIZATION TYPES

- *Type 0: Sub-global Culture*

    - This is where we are right now. We are able to harness the resources of our home planet, but not to its fullest extent.

- *Type I: Planetary Culture*

    - A civilization at this level can harness all the energy available on the planet.

    - This culture should be able to control the weather, earthquakes, and other natural phenomena.

- *Type II: Stellar Culture*

  - At this level a culture would be able to control the energy coming from its star.

  - They would possess technology that enables the control of the orbits of planets and harvest any materials from objects within their solar system.

- *Type III: Galactic Culture*

  - A culture at this level can colonize and utilize the energy of an entire galaxy.

- *Type IV: Universal Culture*

  - As we approach God-like status, a universal culture can control energy on the level of the whole universe.

- *Type V: Multiverse Culture*

  - After having mastered your own universe, why not find another and dominate that too?

So you want to rule the universe? At this point we know of only one being who can fill those shoes—God, the Creator of the universe. Let's see what He has to say about any beings at this level:

> *Thus says the Lord, the King of Israel, and his Redeemer, the Lord of hosts: "I am the First and I am the Last; besides Me there is no God. And who can proclaim as I do? Then let him declare it and set it in order for Me, since I appointed the ancient people. And the things that are coming and shall come, let them show these to them. Do not fear, nor be afraid; have I not told you from that time, and declared it? You are My witnesses. Is there a*

God besides Me? Indeed there is no other Rock; I know not one" (Isaiah 44:6-8).

What can we conclude God has to say about the Kardashev scale? We can take it from the highest authority that even He does not know of any being besides Himself who falls into the top type categories of this scale. My first name, Michael, in Hebrew means "Who is like our God?" Psalm 113:5 poses this rhetorical question as an expression of awe and wonder. The answer, of course is that there is no one like our God. Isaiah 45:5-6 states:

> *I am the Lord, and there is no other; there is no God besides Me. I will gird you, though you have not known Me, that they may know from the rising of the sun to its setting that there is none besides Me. I am the Lord, and there is no other.*

I want to personally invite you to get to know this awesome being who is capable of controlling multiverses (if such a thing exists). His plan from before the beginning of time was for you to know Him well. This very universe is the platform that He created for you to have a place in space and time to play a part in His divine scheme. I hope that in the reading of this book you have been challenged to enter fully into the exciting adventure that it is to follow the Creator of the universe. It is my deepest desire that from the concepts you have read in *The Frequency of the Supernatural* you will be empowered to experience all that God has intended for you.

APPENDIX

Dear Reader,

In my research for this book I spent quite a bit of time looking into the life and sayings of Albert Einstein as I referenced a great deal of his thought and influence on the topic of quantum physics. I felt that it was important for you to see the following quotes:

As a child, I received instruction both in the Bible and in the Talmud. I am a Jew, but I am enthralled by the luminous figure of the Nazarene.

...Jesus is too colossal for the pen of phrasemongers, however artful. No man can dispose of Christianity with a *bon mot*.

…No one can read the Gospels without feeling the actual presence of Jesus. His personality pulsates in every word. No myth is filled with such life.[1]

When asked about the above quotes from the magazine article reporting his comments on Christianity, Einstein carefully read the clipping and replied, "That is what I believe."[2]

NOTES

1. George Sylvester Viereck, "What Life Means to Einstein: An Interview by George Sylvester Viereck" The Saturday Evening Post, October 26, 1929) 17.

2. Albert Einstein, qtd. in Denis Brian, *Einstein: A Life* (New York, NY: J. Wiley & Sons, 1997), 278.

RECOMMENDED BOOKS AND ORGANIZATIONS FOR INNER HEALING

The Transformation of the Inner Man
by John Sandford and Paula Sandford

The Ancient Paths
by Craig S. Hill

https://familyfoundations.com

https://www.restoringthefoundations.org

http://bethelsozo.com/ministry-training

OTHER BOOKS BY MICHAEL-DAVID

As It Is in Heaven

ABOUT MICHAEL-DAVID

Michael-David is an inventor, composer/producer, prophetic harpist/psalmist and Renaissance man. With a lifelong passion for technology, astronomy, and quantum physics, he merges these fields with a love of music and God. His patented electronic harp called the *Harpella* has taken him around the world in prophetic harp music ministry.

www.michael-david.org

www.harptronics.com

The Frequency of the Supernatural is ideal for group studies and has a free companion study guide that can be downloaded as a PDF at

www.michael-david.org/studyguide

There you will also find for purchase additional copies of the book and a DVD study guide where the author personally introduces each chapter. Study questions and answers are presented in a stimulating interactive menu on the DVD for each chapter.